New Day

C000272050

Edited by **Gordon Giles**   **September–December 2022**

15 The Chambers, Vineyard
Abingdon OX14 3FE
brf.org.uk

Bible Reading Fellowship is a charity (233280) and company
limited by guarantee (301324), registered in England and Wales

ISBN 978 1 80039 132 1

Distributed in Australia by:
MediaCom Education Inc, PO Box 610, Unley, SA 5061
Tel: 1 800 811 311 | admin@mediacom.org.au

Distributed in New Zealand by:
Scripture Union Wholesale, PO Box 760, Wellington 6140
Tel: 04 385 0421 | suwholesale@clear.net.nz

Acknowledgements

Scripture quotations marked with the following abbreviations are taken from
the version shown. **NRSV:** The New Revised Standard Version of the Bible,
Anglicised Edition, copyright © 1989, 1995 by the Division of Christian Education
of the National Council of the Churches of Christ in the USA. Used by permission.
All rights reserved. **NIV:** The Holy Bible, New International Version, Anglicised
edition, copyright © 1979, 1984, 2011 by Biblica. Used by permission of Hodder
& Stoughton Publishers, an Hachette UK company. All rights reserved. 'NIV' is a
registered trademark of Biblica. UK trademark number 1448790. **NEB:** New English
Bible, copyright © Cambridge University Press and Oxford University Press 1961,
1970. All rights reserved. **REB:** Revised English Bible, copyright © Cambridge
University Press and Oxford University Press 1989. All rights reserved. **BCP:** The
Book of Common Prayer, the rights in which are vested in the Crown, reproduced
by permission of the Crown's Patentee, Cambridge University Press. **NLT:** The
Holy Bible, New Living Translation, copyright © 1996, 2004, 2007, 2013. Used by
permission of Tyndale House Publishers, Inc., Carol Stream, Illinois 60188. All rights
reserved. **TLB:** The Living Bible copyright © 1971 by Tyndale House Foundation.
Used by permission of Tyndale House Publishers Inc., Carol Stream, Illinois 60188.
All rights reserved. **MSG:** The Message, copyright © 1993, 1994, 1995, 1996, 2000,
2001, 2002 by Eugene H. Peterson. Used by permission of NavPress. All rights
reserved. Represented by Tyndale House Publishers, Inc.

Lyrics from 'O Christ the same, through all our story's pages' (p. 138), copyright ©
Timothy Dudley-Smith. Used by permission of the author.

A catalogue record for this book is available from the British Library

Printed by Gutenberg Press, Tarxien, Malta

Suggestions for using *New Daylight*

Find a regular time and place, if possible, where you can read and pray undisturbed. Before you begin, take time to be still and perhaps use one of the BRF prayers on page 6. Then read the Bible passage slowly (try reading it aloud if you find it over-familiar), followed by the comment. You can also use *New Daylight* for group study and discussion, if you prefer.

The prayer or point for reflection can be a starting point for your own meditation and prayer. Many people like to keep a journal to record their thoughts about a Bible passage and items for prayer. In *New Daylight* we also note the Sundays and some special festivals from the church calendar, to keep in step with the Christian year.

New Daylight and the Bible

New Daylight contributors use a range of Bible versions, and you will find a list of the versions used opposite. You are welcome to use your own preferred version alongside the passage printed in the notes. This can be particularly helpful if the Bible text has been abridged.

New Daylight affirms that the whole of the Bible is God's revelation to us, and we should read, reflect on and learn from every part of both Old and New Testaments. Usually the printed comment presents a straightforward 'thought for the day', but sometimes it may also raise questions rather than simply providing answers, as we wrestle with some of the more difficult passages of scripture.

New Daylight is also available in a deluxe edition (larger format). Visit your local Christian bookshop or BRF's online shop **brfonline.org.uk**. To obtain a cassette version for the visually impaired, contact Torch Trust for the Blind, Torch House, Torch Way, Northampton Road, Market Harborough LE16 9HL; +44 (0)1858 438260; **info@torchtrust.org**. For a Braille edition, contact St John's Guild, Sovereign House, 12–14 Warwick Street, Coventry CV5 6ET; +44 (0)24 7671 4241; **info@stjohnsguild.org**.

Comment on *New Daylight*

To send feedback, please email **enquiries@brf.org.uk**, phone **+44 (0)1865 319700** or write to the address shown opposite.

Writers in this issue

Amy Boucher Pye is an author, speaker and spiritual director. She's a regular contributor to several devotional publications and her books include *7 Ways to Pray*, *The Living Cross* and *Celebrating Christmas*.

Geoff Lowson is a retired priest living in a small village in the west of County Durham. In addition to parochial ministry, he spent 21 years working for the mission agency USPG.

Michael Mitton works freelance in the areas of spirituality and mission. He is also an honorary canon of Derby Cathedral and is the NSM priest in charge of St Paul's Derby. He is author of *Restoring the Woven Cord* (third edition, BRF, 2019).

Stephen Rand worked with Tearfund and Open Doors, travelling widely. Now retired, he is the part-time web editor for the All Party Parliamentary Group for International Freedom of Religion or Belief.

David Runcorn is a 'free-range priest' involved with ministry training, teaching, support and spiritual direction. His books include *The Gift of Tears* (Canterbury, 2018) and *Love Means Love* (SPCK, 2020). **davidruncorn.com**

Margaret Silf is an ecumenical Christian committed to working across and beyond traditional divisions. She is the author of a number of books for 21st-century spiritual pilgrims and a retreat facilitator. She is a mother and grandmother and lives in North Staffordshire.

Rachel Turner is an author, a speaker and the pioneer of Parenting for Faith. Until March 2022, she led the Parenting for Faith team at BRF, and she presents the Parenting for Faith course, a video-based resource for church groups and individuals.

Sally Welch is the former editor of *New Daylight* and a parish priest of 20 years' standing, having ministered in both rural and urban contexts within the Diocese of Oxford. She is currently the diocesan spirituality adviser and co-director of the Centre for Christian Pilgrimage.

Gordon Giles writes...

 In June 2021, the Cathedrals Cycle Relay took to the roads of England. Setting out from Newcastle, the cyclists headed through York, down to London, where they did the shortest leg, between St Paul's and Southwark, and then followed the ancient pilgrimage route to Canterbury via Rochester before turning west, towards Truro, and then back up the country through Worcester, wending their way via Carlisle back to Newcastle.

While only one person did the whole 2,000-mile route, the challenge lasted 42 days and took in all of England's 42 cathedrals. As well as being a great feat of teamwork, it was an opportunity to raise awareness of physical and mental well-being and psychological health, and a great way to bring people together. Being a relay, a baton was handed on from cathedral to cathedral. It was a beautiful baton, made from bronze to a design by the 13-year-old daughter of Shaun Cutler, who conceived and planned the relay. It featured two sculptured hands reaching towards each other, symbolising the idea that 'some days you need a hand, other days you are called to lend a hand'. This baton was literally 'handed' over at each cathedral as prayers were said and a special candle lit for the remaining days of the cycle pilgrimage.

I am being handed a beautiful baton as I become the editor of *New Daylight*, with this edition being my first. Like cyclists pedalling around the country, I feel that I am not only joining a great team of riders around me, a peloton of preachers, but also am inheriting a great and long tradition, carefully and lovingly curated by David Winter, Naomi Starkey, Sally Welch and others. To these we all owe a huge debt of gratitude, and my special thanks go to Sally, who has so graciously handed the baton on to me. With your prayers and the help of so many contributors, who are not only thoughtful, knowledgeable and informed but also lovely people, we begin together the next leg of an exciting journey with God.

So please do continue to walk with us and enjoy our cycle of readings, in faith and hope and love. And don't hesitate to be in touch to tell us how we are doing, and how you are doing.

With every blessing,

REVD CANON DR GORDON GILES

The BRF Prayer

Almighty God,
you have taught us that your word is a lamp for our feet
and a light for our path. Help us, and all who prayerfully
read your word, to deepen our fellowship with you
and with each other through your love.
And in so doing may we come to know you more fully,
love you more truly, and follow more faithfully
in the steps of your Son Jesus Christ, who lives and reigns
with you and the Holy Spirit, one God forevermore.
Amen

The BRF Centenary Prayer

Gracious God,
we rejoice in this centenary year
that you have grown BRF
from a local network of Bible readers
into a worldwide family of ministries.
Thank you for your faithfulness
in nurturing small beginnings
into surprising blessings.
We rejoice that, from the youngest to the oldest,
so many have encountered your word
and grown as disciples of Christ.
Keep us humble in your service,
ambitious for your glory
and open to new opportunities.
For your name's sake
Amen

Looking forward

When I was at school, some of my sixth-form classmates told me that their world literature course included the book of Revelation as a set text. The idea of studying the last book of the Bible alongside Shakespeare, Homer and Tolstoy is certainly an intriguing and creative one. I was in a different group, so did not have that experience myself, sadly. But it reminds us that, however we think of scripture, we should not overlook what is perhaps less obvious to those of faith than others: the Bible is not only the book of books, it is also a library – a collection of books – and therefore contains within it individual works of literature which stand up to scrutiny and lay claim to be great works in their own right. There are many opinions as to *how* to read the Bible, but it never hurts to remember that each book has an author, whose hand, guided by God, can be seen in the text.

The book of Revelation was written by a man called John. It is not entirely clear which John or whether it is the same John who wrote the letters and/or the gospel bearing that name. Some traditions distinguish between John the Evangelist (of gospel fame) and John the Divine (of Revelation fame). When we read any book, novel, biography or whatever, we often want to know about the author – their circumstances, political views and life story. Speculation aside, this information is not really available to us, so the 'John' we meet in Revelation is the author *in* the work, as well as the author *of* the work.

Whoever he was, John was a visionary, clearly inspired and influenced by the Spirit of God. He was also someone of his time and someone who knew the book of Daniel, as well as the geography of what was then known as Asia Minor (modern Turkey). He was a unique person who wrote a unique book, unlike any other in the New Testament and unrivalled in world literature.

For the next ten days join me on a journey of hope through John's opening four chapters. The summer holidays are not quite over yet, so allow me to take you on an armchair pilgrimage, which, in the company of John, will culminate in eternal, heavenly worship.

GORDON GILES

Look who's coming!

Look! He is coming with the clouds; every eye will see him, even those who pierced him; and on his account all the tribes of the earth will wail. So it is to be. Amen. 'I am the Alpha and the Omega,' says the Lord God, who is and who was and who is to come, the Almighty. I, John… was on the island called Patmos because of the word of God and the testimony of Jesus.

John prefaces his visionary letters with a greeting. This was conventional by the standards of the time. The modern gift of email may have enabled us to lose sight of formal greetings, by which we might enquire of someone's good health, send our best wishes and offer some words of encouragement before getting down to the business or purpose of the letter. In the first century it was customary to invoke one's favourite gods. New Testament letter writers Christianised this tradition. John adds this hymn-like verse, which reminded his readers of Daniel 7:13 and reminds us of Charles Wesley's great Advent hymn 'Lo, he comes with clouds descending'. Wesley (1707–88) was himself inspired by a more fiery hymn, also based on Revelation 1:7, by John Cennick (1718–55): 'Lo! He cometh, countless trumpets.'

When we see these words, we may feel in familiar territory, paved in familiar words, a soft opening to the strangeness that will follow. Yet this is no comfort zone – early Christianity was imbued with the idea that Jesus Christ, crucified, risen, ascended and glorified, would soon return, on clouds as referred to in Matthew's gospel and predicted by Daniel. John reminds them to look out for it, and reminds us that this was a real fear, a real expectation and a real hope. Combined with this is the idea that Christ is already among them, so for John and for his readers, whom he instructs, admonishes and encourages, Christ is both 'now' and 'not yet'.

Two thousand years have passed and we still harbour this conundrum: living with Christ in our hearts, but also anticipating his return. Every Advent season brings this home to us, but the return of Christ, and the anticipation and hope it brings, are not just for Advent, but for every day.

Jesus Christ, for whose return we wait in hope,
be with us in spirit this very day. Amen

GORDON GILES

Setting out in sevens

I saw seven golden lampstands, and in the midst of the lampstands I saw one like the Son of Man... He placed his right hand on me, saying... 'As for the mystery of the seven stars that you saw in my right hand, and the seven golden lampstands: the seven stars are the angels of the seven churches, and the seven lampstands are the seven churches.'

The first three chapters of Revelation are known as the 'letters to the seven churches', and are mini epistles that address issues pertinent to their recipients. We can also read them as a little travelogue, a virtual tour of those far-flung outposts of first-century Christian faith. It is possible to visit these places today, although it involves some gruelling bus journeys around western Turkey. It is not for the faint-hearted, and we can get a pretty good view in our mind's eye by reading John's out-tray.

On our armchair travels through Asia Minor we must also travel by numbers. The number seven is our guide. The idea that seven is an almost magical divine number is well known, but it is a residue of a much greater reliance in the ancient world on sacred, cosmic numbers and letters. Three is the number of God, four of the universe (there are four seasons). Seven is the sum of three and four so it is the number of perfection. Thus six, the number below it, is the number of the anti-Christ, of imperfection, of deception.

Nowadays we still have a residue of this. We like phone numbers that begin 0777 or numberplates with 777, and we are averse to three sixes (the famous 'number of the beast' in Revelation 13:18, seen by many as a perfect number of imperfections) and 13. While this makes the numerology of Revelation accessible, we have moved a long way from being superstitious and living our lives by numbers. To John and his readers, however, it was obvious. When we read of the seven letters to seven churches in the shadow of seven lampstands delivered by seven angels and seven stars, what we have is a depiction of supreme divinity painted by holy numbers.

Holy God, help us to travel in wisdom and love
by the light of your sevenfold glory. Amen

GORDON GILES

Ephesus

'To the angel of the church in Ephesus write… "I know your works, your toil and your patient endurance. I know that you cannot tolerate evil-doers; you have tested those who claim to be apostles but are not, and have found them to be false. I also know that you are enduring patiently and bearing up for the sake of my name, and that you have not grown weary. But I have this against you, that you have abandoned the love you had at first.'

We begin our virtual bus ride around Asia Minor at Ephesus, a city second only in significance to Rome. We are guided, not guarded, by angels.

Each church has an angel in Revelation, and angel simply means 'messenger'. This reminds me of the 'flying angel', the emblem of The Mission to Seafarers, the Christian charity supporting those at sea. The angel flies with the gospel to all nations (Revelation 14:6). There are a lot of angels flying about in this book, and they deliver messages of hope, joy and sometimes rebuke. In a contemporary context, I have noticed that one particular diocese names its email servers Gabriel and Raphael, the electronic message servers who deliver all those ecclesiastical emails to clergy and staff alike!

Like angels themselves, John's message to the Ephesian church (to whom Paul wrote a longer letter) is two-edged. Have you ever received feedback that begins with something positive and then hurts? The conversation begins with 'This was good', and then comes the 'but'. The Ephesians are told, you are working hard, not without success… *but…* you have abandoned the authentic love that established you in faith. Ouch!

When we read these mini epistles, we should read them against ourselves, just as we do Paul's longer ones. We might be good at reading the Bible *for* ourselves, but poor at reading it *against* ourselves. When John accuses the Ephesians of losing their original love, might we stand accused too? On this bumpy bus ride, we arrive at Ephesus to be asked, 'Do you still love the Lord your God with all your heart?' Has it gone a bit stale, covered in the cares and issues of our day, the little things that seem so big, and the big things that are actually so small?

Lord Jesus, renew a right and loving spirit within me. Amen

GORDON GILES

Smyrna

'I know your affliction and your poverty, even though you are rich. I know the slander on the part of those who say that they are Jews and are not, but are a synagogue of Satan. Do not fear what you are about to suffer… Be faithful until death, and I will give you the crown of life.'

Our next stop is now called İzmir, a popular tourist destination 50 miles north of Ephesus. The oldest part dates from the eleventh century BC, but a 'new' Smyrna grew up after the fourth century BC. It became a wealthy Roman seaport with a large Jewish community. Smyrna means 'myrrh'.

John offers reassurance to this persecuted church, telling them that true wealth is not commercial but spiritual. Just as the Jewish leaders in Jerusalem had provoked the Roman authorities to execute Jesus, the synagogue leaders in Smyrna were doing the same to his followers. So there is trouble ahead and not only for ten days. A young man of Smyrna at the time, Polycarp, was later to become bishop there, but was martyred by an unholy alliance of Jews and pagans in AD153.

Persecution of Christians is neither new nor short-lived. The Middle East today is not a safe place for Christians, who a century ago comprised 20 per cent of the region's population but now constitute barely more than three per cent. Changes in the political order in the region and the rise of extremist ideologies have undermined co-existence, and Christians are often victims of violence, harassment, expulsion, destruction of cultural and religious heritage, and larceny, and they may be banned from worshipping. Arrests and imprisonment of religious leaders and the criminalisation of Christian education have all been reported in recent years.

If we think that Christianity is sometimes marginalised or scorned in our part of the world, and glibly use the word 'persecution', as some do, it is time to turn our gaze on the plight of those few Christians left in the Middle East, whose presence is unwelcome and whose suffering overlooked or ignored by the rest of the world. Persecution is not a thing of the past, but a real presence in need of awareness-raising, prayer and action.

God, we pray for peace in the Holy Land
and for freedom of religion worldwide. Amen

GORDON GILES

Pergamum

'You are holding fast to my name, and you did not deny your faith in me even in the days of Antipas my witness, my faithful one, who was killed among you, where Satan lives. But… you also have some who hold to the teaching of the Nicolaitans. Repent then. If not, I will come to you soon and make war against them with the sword of my mouth.'

Welcome to Pergamum, an old Greek capital which turned to the worship of Rome as a deity in its own right. Any new religion focused on Jesus Christ was inevitably going to have difficulty there. Some Christians under threat of capital punishment, which their friend Antipas had endured, were inclined to follow the Nicolaitans' self-preserving accommodation of pagan practices and idolisation of Rome. This brief letter highlights the dilemma: evade Roman persecution by all means, only to endure the 'sword' of Christ's verbal judgement.

It is awful to see people suffer for political or religious belief. In countries such as Myanmar, China, Russia and elsewhere, speaking out or taking a stand is incredibly dangerous. Complain as we do about referenda, leaders and political parties, most of us have no idea what it is like to find that what we say or think could get us killed, judicially or surreptitiously. There are millions of people who live under restricted freedoms of speech, conscience or religion, and we must pray for them and support their rights as best we can.

There are also those who have faith or hold honest views who do not dare speak out or bring attention to themselves, preferring to blend in or keep their heads down. They are not cowards. They are like you or me. What would you do if speaking out could bring personal danger not only to yourself but also to family members, friends and colleagues? Dietrich Bonhoeffer, who was martyred by the Nazis only a few days before World War II ended, said in his book *The Cost of Discipleship* that Christ bids us to come and die. It has been the case since first-century Pergamum and is still the case now. Could you do that? Would you?

Jesus, you call us to live and die for you. Help those who must. Amen

GORDON GILES

Thyatira

'I know your works – your love, faith, service, and patient endurance… But… you tolerate that woman Jezebel, who calls herself a prophet and is teaching and beguiling my servants to practise fornication and to eat food sacrificed to idols… I am the one who searches minds and hearts, and I will give to each of you as your works deserve… To the one who conquers I will also give the morning star.'

Like Pergamum, Thyatiran Christians were beset with the problem of how to blend in with pagan culture. In this hometown of the merchant Lydia, whom Paul meets in Acts 16, the stakes were lower, but there was still an issue about generally 'joining in' with idolatrous eating and immoral behaviour which others took for granted (and from which converts were being asked to disengage). The guilds of Thyatira were basically pagan in nature and culture, thereby putting any Christian involved in commerce in an awkward position, which could lead to loss of status, wealth or influence. Meanwhile others, inspired by the woman whom the author calls Jezebel, did not consider it to be a problem.

Yesterday we reflected on Christ's call to stand up for our faith, even unto death. Commercial martyrdom is less painful but more prevalent: to what extent should the business practices and social and working lives of Christians be governed by allegiance to Christ if compromised? Are there trades in which Christians should not engage, invest or operate? Many would suggest arms-dealing, alcohol, tobacco or fossil fuels. Others would debate this or disagree (which proves the point and highlights the difficulty). Modern slavery is still a worldwide phenomenon and is hard to avoid, albeit inadvertently or unknowingly, as it can impinge on basic activities such as agriculture. It is so easy in this day and age to be unwittingly compromised by the connections we have, the company we keep or the things we consume.

The lure of the Jezebel of profit can cloud our vision or beguile us to turn a blind eye. We might even be persuaded that it is best not to ask too many questions or know the answers. Welcome to Thyatira.

Lord, give us integrity to live for you. Amen

GORDON GILES

Sardis

'You have a name of being alive, but you are dead. Wake up, and strengthen what remains... for I have not found your works perfect in the sight of my God. Remember then what you received and heard; obey it, and repent. If you do not wake up, I will come like a thief, and you will not know at what hour I will come to you. Yet you have still a few people in Sardis who have not soiled their clothes.'

Sardis was a complacent city in Lydia, which had endured being invaded at night twice. The Christians there were mostly accused of laziness, forgetfulness and not putting faith into action. Their good reputation was undeserved. The call to 'wake up' relates to Jesus' analogy of the thief in the night (Luke 12:39; 1 Thessalonians 5:2) and the direct experience of defeat in nocturnal attacks.

This identification of a complacent church, concerned with its reputation, has modern overtones. Many failures of church leaders (and media and sporting organisations, too) relating to safeguarding young people and vulnerable adults have come to light. Common threads are complacency and reputation. The two are linked: the church is not necessarily full of 'good' people, and only terrible revelations in recent years have forced the church to understand and grapple with the dire consequences of turning a blind eye to severe, real allegations.

There are now signs of wakefulness. The call from victims, survivors and those who have listened for the church to wake up to safeguarding is being heard. The church needs to heed what is now being received, and obey it. The culture is slowly changing. Not everyone is soiled by it. But just as the letter to Sardis is a warning both to the complacent and to those who are not, so is the message about safeguarding something which is for all.

This is not simply a modern phenomenon, for safeguarding the vulnerable lies at the heart of the gospel, which is good news for the weak and those who are persecuted and abused. Safeguarding is for everyone, and everyone needs to be involved in ensuring that complacency and reputational risk do not hold sway, as they did in Sardis.

God, preserve us from complacency and protect all your children. Amen

GORDON GILES

Philadelphia

'I know your works. Look, I have set before you an open door, which no one is able to shut. I know that you have but little power, and yet you have kept my word and have not denied my name... I will keep you from the hour of trial that is coming on the whole world to test the inhabitants of the earth. I am coming soon.'

Known today as Alaşehir, ancient Philadelphia was originally named after 'one who loved his brother' at its foundation by King Eumenes II of Pergamon. To its people, John offers hope in the expectation of the return of Christ, through an 'open door' and avoidance of the ensuing tribulations. Of all the seven churches, Philadelphia is most to be praised and encouraged.

In a world in which churches seem to compete, it is good to be reminded that rebuke is not the only language of scripture, nor indeed of modern life. It is easy and common to denigrate or complain about other congregations. John gives credit where credit is due, and so should we all. Contexts and circumstances vary, and yet when Christians rival one another they often apply their own contexts on to another's and make comparisons.

For example, in some denominations, each church contributes to the running of the diocese. Yet, without knowing the situation, some compare and complain. Ultimately Christian communities stand before God, not each other. Many struggle to pay bills or grow congregations. In first-century Turkey, however, the measure was not about 'success' or viability, but about withstanding persecution. The churches who received John's encyclical would have noticed how Philadelphia merited encouragement rather than criticism.

Is your church 'better' than so-and-so's? Is the preaching or music or fellowship better? Is the congregation larger or the minister a nicer person? Faith is not a competition, and Philadelphia – the very name of this persecuted, praiseworthy first-century Christian community – helps us. For we are called by Christ to love our brothers and sisters, to encourage and build them up, keeping open the door of fellowship and support.

God, may the doors of all your churches always be open in faith,
hope and love. Amen

GORDON GILES

Laodicea

'I know your works; you are neither cold nor hot. I wish that you were either cold or hot. So, because you are lukewarm, and neither cold nor hot, I am about to spit you out of my mouth. For you say, "I am rich, I have prospered, and I need nothing"… Listen! I am standing at the door, knocking; if you hear my voice and open the door, I will come in to you and eat with you, and you with me.'

Lying 63 miles south-east of Philadelphia, Laodicea (now Denizli) was also prone to earthquakes and was almost completely destroyed in AD60. But the population declined Roman help to rebuild, preferring to do it themselves. It was a wealthy city with large Jewish and Christian congregations. The lure of wealth and inclination to profess the faith but not do very much about it must have been strong, exactly as it is in so many comfortable places today.

These words to the Laodiceans are famous for their evocation of lukewarm food or drink. Hot coffee is lovely and iced coffee delicious, but who wants tepid, off-the-boil insipidness? It annoys John: one knows how to handle those who do not walk in the way, and how to praise those who do, but those who are neither here nor there – yuck!

Many people keep their head down and get on with life: going to church when it suits, putting something in the collection plate and confining faith to a Sunday activity. Yet the kettle of faith, hope and love needs to be boiled every day. Our church coffee needs to be hot and caffeinated with the power of the Spirit. You can't make a decent cuppa with warm water.

Christ comes to eat and drink with us when we are faithful. We encounter him in the Eucharist, at which we celebrate not only Christ's body and blood sacrifice in the bread and wine, but also our own calling to *be* the body of Christ. The cold bread and wine of Communion is made hot with spiritual fire, and as we, the body of Christ, take the body-bread of Christ into our own bodies, we are fed with daily, spiritual bread for our ongoing pilgrimage.

Lord, warm our hearts with your living bread
that we may be hot in your service. Amen

GORDON GILES

The heavenly worship

'I will show you what must take place after this.' At once I was in the spirit, and there in heaven stood a throne, with one seated on the throne!... 'Holy, holy, holy, the Lord God the Almighty, who was and is and is to come'... 'You are worthy, our Lord and God, to receive glory and honour and power, for you created all things, and by your will they existed and were created.'

Our journey around the seven churches has been a bit of a rough ride through terrain of heavy criticism and threats of judgement. But now we have reached a heavenly destination, where with saints, angels and all the company of heaven we can join in the holy praise of God. This is the destiny of all prayer and praise and the hope to which we aspire, both during and after the here and now. God is at the centre, not only of this scene of worship, but of the whole book of Revelation.

The resonances of this worship scene are from the Old Testament (the 'Holy, holy' was not new) and would be familiar to Jewish readers. Also familiar to Christians down the ages, it is not hard to envisage this scene in our favourite church building. Nor is it inappropriate, for in worship we strive to join our songs and praises with those who have gone before us and who worship God in another dimension.

This includes those yet to be born, whose liturgies and hymns will combine with ours. When we sing a hymn, for example, we join our voices, not only with those who have sung it in the past but also with those who are yet to sing it. Much of what we sing or say in worship has ancient precedent and resonance, but there is also room for spontaneity and creativity and the whole gamut of praise is encompassed historically, globally and futuristically.

Remember that when you praise God: we are unique, but never alone. Time and space and sound and sight are embraced and enfolded by a great divine presence, here, there and everywhere, offered to God in Trinity: Father, Son and Holy Spirit, now and always.

O Holy Trinity, by your mercy, may our earthbound worship be worthy
to offer at your heavenly throne. Amen

GORDON GILES

Tell it to your children

The first time I went abseiling, I was terrified. My dad felt that knowing how to lower yourself off a cliff edge was an essential life skill, and so at nine years old, I found myself strapped into a harness looking down a very long drop to the ground. My father's friends had been up and down multiple times already, but my whole body was shaking with fear at the thought of doing it myself. They all seemed so confident. No worry, no doubt. They completely trusted their equipment and seemed to delight in leaping into the unknown on a rope, knowing they would be safe. I was not so sure. The rope looked so small. The knots didn't look tight enough. No matter how much my dad told me to trust him and the equipment, I struggled to find the courage to lean into the void.

Our future can often feel like a cliff edge. What comes next is unknown, and all we have to cling to is a rope of faith that God will be there whatever comes next. But knowing the truth of God's presence doesn't always translate into a faith-filled peace.

The people in the Bible were in the same position: Moses, Joshua, Ruth, the disciples, Mary. We may sometimes overlook their pain because we have confidence in how their stories ended. We know that God rescued, restored, provided or produced a miracle. But they didn't know that. Their lives were in crisis, and they were facing the empty void of the future, not knowing what would happen next.

Hebrews 11 lists numerous 'Heroes of the faith'. Many of those listed are heroes not because of any significant works they did, but for how they confidently walked into the future with God, not knowing what was coming. They just knew that the rope they held on to was strong and would guide them safely through it. Like these heroes of faith, we are still in the middle of our stories, not knowing what will come next. Over the next week, we will be exploring how we can walk forward and trust that God will be with us always in this unknown future we face.

RACHEL TURNER

The 'what ifs'

Moses said to God, 'If I come to the Israelites and say to them, "The God of your ancestors has sent me to you", and they ask me, "What is his name?" what shall I say to them?' God said to Moses, 'I am who I am.' He said further, 'Thus you shall say to the Israelites, "I am has sent me to you… The Lord, the God of your ancestors, the God of Abraham, the God of Isaac, and the God of Jacob, has sent me to you": This is my name for ever, and this my title for all generations.'

I am a planner. I love the feeling when everything in my head is beautifully organised into a plan that I and others can follow: charts, lists, calendars and Post-it notes are my weapons to face the uncertain future. I want to thoroughly cover the 'What ifs' that may arise, so I can be prepared if and when it happens. It makes me feel safe.

The reading for today is a small snippet of a much longer conversation Moses was having with God. God had chosen Moses to be God's messenger and leader of the Israelites out of slavery. Moses appeared to have a severe case of the 'What ifs': What if I'm not good enough? What if they ask what your name is? What if I can't speak well enough? What if they do not believe me? What if they do listen and then don't think you were God?

I sometimes want God to play my planning game too. I want him to lay out the future for me in clarity so that I can feel safe. But he often gives me what he gave Moses: assurance of his presence. God's response every time to Moses was to assure Moses that he would be with him, guide him and even work miracles and teach Moses what to say. Sometimes he gave specifics, and sometimes he didn't. God was insistent that Moses' security and trust should be in his ability to guide Moses in all that would come – to trust that God would walk into the future with him and help him every step of the way.

Do I trust that God will do that for me? When I look at the future, am I sure that God is already there, with everything I need to walk into it? Do I trust that he will help and guide me every step of the way?

God, fill my heart with confidence in you. Help me see and hear you more, that I may know your presence and guidance every step of my future.

RACHEL TURNER

Weaving a future

After staying there for a considerable time, Paul said farewell to the believers and sailed for Syria, accompanied by Priscilla and Aquila. At Cenchreae he had his hair cut, for he was under a vow. When they reached Ephesus, he left them there, but first he himself went into the synagogue and had a discussion with the Jews. When they asked him to stay longer, he declined; but on taking leave of them, he said, 'I will return to you, if God wills.'

When I miscarried our first child, I was devastated. It felt like such an ending, a heart-wrenching finale of a hope. It was hard trying to figure out how to keep moving forward or be optimistic about the future.

Priscilla and Aquila are some of my favourite people in scripture. They were happily living in Rome, with a family and a business, when their life was suddenly destroyed. The Roman emperor had banished the Jewish community from Rome, forcing Priscilla and Aquila to flee from all they had known. They must have felt like their future was stolen from them. They landed in Corinth, across the sea, and tried to carve out a life as tentmakers.

Along came the apostle Paul, looking for a place to live and work as he built the church in Corinth and found friendship with Priscilla and Aquila. They hosted Paul and were among the founders of the Corinthian church, leading within their home. God took a tragedy and wove it into a beautiful and fruitful future. He didn't change the past but brought good out of it. In this passage, they travelled with Paul to Ephesus, presumably to help plant the church with Paul. But once again, it didn't work out how they thought it would. And yet, it was just as fruitful.

Our past does not dictate the good that God can bring in the future. He finds ways of bringing 'beauty instead of ashes' (Isaiah 61:3, NIV) and causing all things to 'work together for good to those who love God' (Romans 8:28, NIV footnote).

God is drawing us into a beautiful future with goodness in it, even out of loss or uncertainty. We can trust that, even when we can't see it yet.

God, only you see the good you will bring out of my past and present.
I trust you to weave a future for me.

RACHEL TURNER

The guiding of a shepherd

The Lord is my shepherd, I shall not want. He makes me lie down in green pastures; he leads me beside still waters; he restores my soul. He leads me in right paths for his name's sake… Surely goodness and mercy shall follow me all the days of my life, and I shall dwell in the house of the Lord my whole life long.

Whenever I read Psalm 23, I pictured a British shepherd standing in a lush green field watching his sheep grazing by a river. It looked fantastic in my head. I kept asking God, 'When do we get to the field bit? When do I get to just rest in a beautiful, peaceful place and do nothing but feast? Give me that future, God!'

But the writer of this psalm was David, a shepherd in the wilderness of Israel. When we look at how he would have shepherded, it paints a very different picture of the future we have with God.

The grass wasn't in one field, but were tufts between dust and rocks. He led his sheep to a place to feed and rest, and then would have to move them on to the next field, and the next and the next. He knew the route to the best fields and where to lead his sheep to find water in the desert. The sheep's future wasn't about finding one happy place and staying put. Their happy future was in staying close to a shepherd who would continually lead them to temporary areas of feeding and rest and then bring them to the next place.

God promises to lead us to places of refreshing. He knows where to take us to give us what we need to flourish. Our job is to stay close to the God who promises to take us to where he knows we need to go. We persevere in the desert of our present because we know he is leading us somewhere. When we lose that sense of following a God who cares for us, our future feels terrifying. But our shepherd is there, ready to guide us into our next field of refreshing and move us on when it is right.

God, make me sensitive to your guiding and help me see behind me the path of how you have brought me from place to place. Give me peace in the desert.

RACHEL TURNER

Confidence in the God who can

Shadrach, Meshach and Abednego answered the king, 'O Nebuchadnez-zar, we have no need to present a defence to you in this matter. If our God whom we serve is able to deliver us from the furnace of blazing fire and out of your hand, O king, let him deliver us. But if not, be it known to you, O king, that we will not serve your gods and we will not worship the golden statue that you have set up.'

When I make decisions, I often get stuck in a loop of logic. I want to know the consequences of each of my options, and if I can't, I am very nervous about making a choice. From university to jobs, the unknown future can be nerve-wracking.

Shadrach, Meshach and Abednego were facing death, and yet whether or not God would rescue them didn't seem to be a stumbling block for their choice. They confidently decided to do what they felt was right, trusting that whatever God chose to do would be fine. They trusted that whether God rescued them from the trial or helped them in it, he would be there, and that was enough for them.

So often, I only want the easy option in my future: the rescue, the saving, the pain-free, easy life. What would it take to be like those three followers of God and say, 'I trust that God can rescue me from this, if he wants to. But even if he doesn't rescue me, I choose a future with him'? What would have to change in me to decide, whether God heals me of this cancer or not, I will choose to walk the journey with him? Whether he gets my child into the school she wants, I will look for him in the decision and what he is doing in it? Whether he miraculously delivers me from my financial troubles or not, I will draw close to God?

Shadrach, Meshach and Abednego were committed to a future with God, and he stood with them in the fire and talked with them face to face. May we all be so bold as to walk into the future, eager for however God wants to go with us.

God, fill me with confidence in your presence in my future. I trust you.
However you choose to be with me, I say yes and thank you.

RACHEL TURNER

The power of your stories

We will not hide them from their descendants; we will tell the next generation the praiseworthy deeds of the Lord, his power, and the wonders he has done… so that the next generation would know them, even the children yet to be born, and they in turn would tell their children. Then they would put their trust in God and would not forget his deeds but would keep his commands.

'We' is a powerful word. It implies a sense of belonging, of togetherness. To be no longer alone but part of a bigger group. We all need that. There are things that we can do together that we simply cannot do alone.

Children and young people are vital members of our current church and are also the next generation to rise up and run with faith, in turn discipling and encouraging the next generation who will, in their time, rise up the next. But to step into their future, scripture says they need us. How do we help them do that? By being 'we'.

This growing generation needs our stories – stories of God in our ordinary, everyday lives; stories of God when we are grieving, pioneering, in hidden seasons or in the biggest moments of our lives. They need to hear of God's faithfulness and how to find him in places of imperfection, loss and fear. Some of us connect with God through logic and science, some of us through art and music. Some of us love boisterous worship, and some of us value silence and ritual. We all connect with God in different ways, learn in different ways, pray in different ways – but we all are loved by the same God. Our children need stories of who God is in all life's circumstances and of how to find him no matter what shape they are.

If we are looking forward to our future, the power of our God stories may resonate for centuries to come through the lives of those we share our stories with.

God, make me bold to share my stories with the next generation, that they may find you in their ordinary lives because of who you are in mine.

RACHEL TURNER

Ordinary everyday

Jesus came to them and said, 'All authority in heaven and on earth has been given to me. Therefore go and make disciples of all nations, baptising them in the name of the Father and of the Son and of the Holy Spirit, and teaching them to obey everything I have commanded you. And surely I am with you always, to the very end of the age.'

When I picture the scene of Jesus' final moments with his disciples, it plays like a movie in my head. Dramatic music swells as the wind whips at Jesus' perfect curls, and his strong voice echoes across the valley. It is a grand pronouncement, a weighty calling.

I often read that last sentence as conditional; as they go and do what he told them to do, he would be with them. But I wonder if 'Surely I am with you always' meant something else too, something much more personal.

Jesus had spent the past three years being with that group of people. They travelled, camped and ate together. They talked about their hopes and dreams, and experienced grief together. They laughed, shared stories and jokes, and danced at celebrations together. They were bored on long trips together, and they learned each other's quirks and what brought each other joy. Jesus was their companion and friend.

When Jesus gave them this mighty Great Commission, I'm sure they felt the spiritual weight of it. But in that last sentence, I see not just the Son of God assuring his disciples of his continued presence and power as they accomplish great things; I also see Jesus assuring the people he loved that he would continue to be their companion and friend in their ordinary, everyday life.

Our futures are full of the ordinary every day: job, tasks, laundry, chores. We work out the Great Commission in talking to neighbours and colleagues and how we live with God in our homes. Jesus promises us that he will be with us in the midst of every moment of it as a companion and friend. Whatever our future holds, he will be there to share it with us. Let's be willing to share it with him.

Jesus, thank you that you are here with me right now. Hear my heart, and help me stay aware of your companionship and friendship.

RACHEL TURNER

Jesus Christ is the same yesterday and today and forever

God has said, 'Never will I leave you; never will I forsake you.' So we say with confidence, 'The Lord is my helper; I will not be afraid. What can mere mortals do to me?' Remember your leaders, who spoke the word of God to you. Consider the outcome of their way of life and imitate their faith. Jesus Christ is the same yesterday and today and forever.

When I was at the cliff edge with my father, everything in me was telling me that the rope wouldn't hold me or that the equipment would fail. But my father was telling me to trust and follow his directions. In my head, my life was in danger. But then I thought about my history with my dad. How he loved me and how protective he was of me. My experience with my dad told me that I should trust him. The same dad who kept me safe in the past was the same one who would protect my future. And so I jumped off a cliff.

Jesus is the same yesterday, today and forever, unchangeable and faithful. God who loves and rescued us in the past waits for us in our future. The same God who sat with us in our pain is lovingly ready to celebrate our joy in the future.

We all have past experiences with God to be reminded of when needing to summon the courage to step into our tomorrows. We have much scripture to draw on, and we can say to God, 'I trust that you will be this for me too!' One particular time, when I felt like I needed to pray for my future, I wrote down on a piece of paper all the scripture I could think of that spoke of who God was, and I added little notes of stories from my past of when he was those things for me. I put it on the ground and stood on the paper that represented the truth of who God was yesterday and today to pray for the future.

There are times when we need to remind ourselves of who will be with us in the future, so we can jump off the cliff into our tomorrows, holding fast on to the rope of our faith in the God who never changes.

God, remind us all of who you are, that we may boldly seek you in all our tomorrows.

RACHEL TURNER

Unfamiliar voices of the Old Testament

There will be a variety of reasons why a story, text or insight in the Bible is unfamiliar to us. We may have simply not read it before; perhaps the Bible is still new to us – and there is a lot of it! But even the most faithful Bible readers know those times when a text or verse startles us, and we sit there thinking, 'How have I never noticed that verse before?' The Bible never stops surprising us.

Sometimes a familiar verse or story that we thought we understood well speaks to us in new and unexpected ways. Possibly our previous understanding lacked some important background. Or we had been making our own assumptions or bringing our own biases about what the text meant. Church history has many such examples of this. The Bible always has more to teach and reveal to us.

The readings for the next fortnight are, of course, a personal selection. They come from all corners of the Old Testament, and the themes range widely. They can only be brief encounters taken from the midst of larger and often complex narratives and contexts, so they find their place and voice as part of a bigger picture.

As I have explored these 'unfamiliar voices', one feature has constantly challenged me. It is the sheer earthy, unvarnished honesty of Hebrew writing in all its forms. The scriptures refuse to smooth out or explain the theological sharp edges and awkwardness in the lives and events they describe. This challenges us to resist reaching for the answers too quickly and simply. We need to linger with the questions. It also calls us to welcome the strangeness of these voices, to be open to their unfamiliar insights and to follow when they lead us on unexpected paths.

In my comments I have tried to honour this. I offer some reflections and explanations but have otherwise tried to keep out of the way. I have tried to leave space for the sometimes unsettling, even disturbing, encounters with texts, personalities and stories, and so to hear God speaking in unfamiliar ways. Truly, 'God speaks to us in a thousand voices' (Hugh Prather, 1938–2010) and invites us into conversation with them all.

DAVID RUNCORN

Voices of creation

The heavens are telling the glory of God; and the firmament proclaims his handiwork. Day to day pours forth speech, and night to night declares knowledge. There is no speech, nor are there words; their voice is not heard; yet their voice goes out through all the earth, and their words to the end of the world.

The psalmist is hearing voices. Were they on the wind? In the clouds? Flowing through the energy of the river?

Jesus tells us to pay attention to creation: 'Look at the birds… Consider the lilies' (Matthew 6:26, 28). But in relating to the created world, Christians have tended to swing between two extremes. One is to be sentimental. The other is to see the material world as fallen and sinful and to prioritise the 'spiritual' instead. The Bible does neither. In this psalm, as elsewhere in the Old Testament, creation is all God intends it to be. It is alive in the sheer delight of God's creating presence. Its voice is a torrent of endless, joyful praise to God and *about* God. There is nowhere it cannot be heard. The ancient theologians spoke of creation as the first Bible.

Gerard Manley Hopkin's poetry is full of wonder at a world 'charged' with God's presence. Thomas Traherne insisted we need a deeper relationship with the created world if we are to know our own place in it and recognise God there: 'You never enjoy the world aright, till the Sea itself floweth in your veins, till you are clothed with the heavens, and crowned with the stars. Till you can sing and rejoice and delight in God.' Julian of Norwich meditated on a hazel nut in the palm of her hand. In its existence, its life and sustaining, she met the fullness of God. Oliver Clément said, 'To contemplate the smallest object is to experience the Trinity.'

There has never been a more urgent time to rediscover all this. Everything is at stake. In this psalm, without speech or words, unfamiliar voices are calling, moment by moment. They call us to notice, to wonder, to worship – and to join a holy life partnership with all creation, to the praise of God.

Lord, help me listen to the voices of creation.

DAVID RUNCORN

I have no voice

Now the word of the Lord came to me saying, 'Before I formed you in the womb I knew you… I appointed you a prophet to the nations.' Then I said, 'Ah, Lord God! Truly I do not know how to speak, for I am only a boy.' But the Lord said to me, 'Do not say, "I am only a boy"'… Then the Lord put out his hand and touched my mouth; and the Lord said to me, 'Now I have put my words in your mouth.'

Sometimes the unfamiliar voice is our own. Not, in the first instance, what we may say to others, but what we say and affirm about ourselves. For reasons of fearfulness or lack of confidence we all have voices within us that are silent, so we are not familiar with them. They have yet to be heard.

I recall the struggles of someone being strongly encouraged to believe God was calling her to ordained ministry. The idea awakened deep fears in her. Some of it was rooted in unhelpful relationships in her past where her voice was regularly mocked and silenced. It was hard to believe what God might be saying to her. Even harder was to find the voice within to say 'Yes' and to begin to talk to God about his loving call to her. It began as a whisper but slowly grew louder. She hesitantly and bravely grew into the person God was calling her to be and began to speak with the voice she did not know was within her.

Jeremiah's first response to God's call was to say, 'I cannot speak.' I have no voice. Moses said something similar. But God's call does not overpower or dominate. As we respond and grow into his loving purpose for us, we are growing into who we truly are. We begin to speak with our own voice. And, as with Jeremiah and the prophets, God's call comes with the promise of his sustaining and enabling.

God knows us and who we may become in his call. The challenge is to trust. To let him touch our mouth and to begin to speak with the voice that is truly ours.

Lord, touch my mouth. Give me voice.

DAVID RUNCORN

The hesitant voice

Now the donkeys of Kish, Saul's father, had strayed. So Kish said to his son Saul, 'Take one of the boys with you; go and look for the donkeys'… They passed through the land of Shaalim, but they were not there [and] the land of Benjamin, but they did not find them. When they came to the land of Zuph, Saul said to the boy who was with him, 'Let us turn back, or my father will stop worrying about the donkeys and worry about us.'

One of the devices in Hebrew storytelling is to make the first words a person speaks a clue to their particular character. This does not mean they cannot change. Rather it suggests what they have to offer, or will need to find, to face whatever tasks will be theirs. Samuel's first words were 'Here I am' (1 Samuel 3:4). And he would indeed be utterly present to God and his people throughout his life. Those words define him.

This story of the young Saul and the lost donkeys comes just before he is chosen to be king of Israel. Saul's first words? 'Let us turn back.' The storyteller is offering a clue as to what might follow. For throughout his life and kingship, Saul was unable to see anything through. He kept turning back. Saul needed to learn another response to life. But it eluded him. It remained an unspoken, unfamiliar, voice.

What might he have said instead? What other responses could he have made? And how might this speak to us? Do you know your 'first words'? These will be your reflex responses when faced with new or sudden challenges? For example, do you tend to move forwards or step back at such moments? Of course, it depends a lot on what we are actually facing. But we develop reflexes. We can play safe or take risks. We can be open to adventure or hold back from the unknown. Where are the challenges for you to 'grow'?

At all times, in the call of God and the gift of life, we choose how we respond. Are there unspoken, unfamiliar voices within us, that might free us to respond, grow and risk in new and exciting ways?

Lord, help me to lean forwards into life and to keep searching until I find.

DAVID RUNCORN

Pharaoh's daughter

The daughter of Pharaoh came to bathe at the river… She saw the basket among the reeds… When she opened it, she saw the child… and she took pity on him. 'This must be one of the Hebrews' children,' she said. Then his sister said to Pharaoh's daughter, 'Shall I go and get you a nurse from the Hebrew women to nurse the child for you?' Pharaoh's daughter said to her, 'Yes'… When the child grew up… Pharaoh's daughter… took him as her son. She named him Moses, 'because', she said, 'I drew him out of the water.'

We know nothing about Pharaoh's daughter – not even her name. But when she happens upon a Hebrew baby, in a basket, caught in the rushes, she subverts her father's policy and adopts him as her own. She may have put herself at risk doing this. God's people would have enjoyed the unintended pun in the name she gave him – Moses, 'I draw out'. For Moses would, in turn, draw God's people out of slavery to freedom.

By her actions, without ever knowing it, she joins a community of women in the scriptures, named and unnamed, whose disobedience and cunning subverts the written scripts and changes history and faith in their world.

Pharaoh's daughter found herself in an unexpected situation that asked immediate but unfamiliar questions of her. Exploring the theme of guidance and choices, Niall Williams writes in his novel *As It Is in Heaven* of 'strange and unknowable conspiracies of the world'. They are those moments when an unexpected situation and our unplanned responses combine to change the outcomes in ways we could never have predicted. Stephen, in that novel, does just that – behaving out of character and with no sense of how significant it would be. He acts out of 'a blind foreknowledge that told him it was the right thing to do'. Perhaps that is what happened on the riverbank that morning.

What we readers know is that woven through this story is the will and purpose of God. The Christian word for this is 'providence'. What if our most significant choices, words and actions are not 'obvious' ones? We may not even know or see the consequence of what we have done. But God does.

Lord, may my words and actions have consequences I never realise.

DAVID RUNCORN

The eyelids of the dawn

'Can you draw out Leviathan with a fish-hook, or press down its tongue with a cord? Can you put a rope in its nose, or pierce its jaw with a hook?… Any hope of capturing it will be disappointed; were not even the gods overwhelmed at the sight of it?… I will not keep silence concerning its limbs, or its mighty strength, or its splendid frame… Its sneezes flash forth light, and its eyes are like the eyelids of the dawn.'

The book of Job reaches its climax in a long, wonderful creation poem in which God celebrates all he has made (Job 38—41). He takes special delight in two creatures: Behemoth and Leviathan. He calls them the first of his greatest acts. In that ancient world they were powerful, untameable, mythical chaos monsters. God teases Job, 'Don't try catching or fishing for them.' But what gives God joy here is something of terror to us. Life has a capacity to tip into such chaos. It is uncontrollable. These monsters are more usually images of evil or fallen creation.

One line here is possibly the most significant in this long, harrowed poem: 'Its eyes are like the eyelids of the dawn,' says God. 'The dawn' is a poetic way to express new beginnings and the passing of darkness. It is an image of hope. Back at the beginning of Job's terrible sufferings, he tipped into despair and cursed the day he was born. Let that day never begin, he says – 'may it not see the eyelids of the morning' (3:9). It is the same image. But here at the far end of the poem, out of a life that has descended into chaotic suffering, that image is repeated, now as a message of unfamiliar hope. Something new will yet dawn out of this – even out of the chaos itself.

There is no easy way to speak faith and hope into the harrowed, undeserved sufferings that can happen in life. Indeed, such attempts are more often hopelessly insensitive. This is no attempted 'happy ending' in Job either. But look, there, where it has been wildest and darkest – is that the first glimpse of the dawn?

Lord, help me glimpse your hope and beginnings, even in chaos.

DAVID RUNCORN

Living in generosity

Ruth the Moabite… gleaned in… the part of the field belonging to Boaz… Boaz said to his servant… 'To whom does this young woman belong?' The servant… answered, 'She is the Moabite who came back with Naomi… She has been on her feet from early this morning until now, without resting even for a moment'… Boaz instructed his young men, 'Let her glean even among the standing sheaves, and do not reproach her… pull out some handfuls for her from the bundles, and leave them for her to glean, and do not rebuke her.'

The book of Ruth begins with famine, exile and multiple bereavements. It ends with homecoming, love and new life. God is almost entirely out of sight in this short story of two widows and a farmer. Only in the final scene is any outcome directly attributed to divine intervention.

When Naomi decides to return to Bethlehem, her young widowed daughter-in-law refuses to leave her. Ruth was under no obligation in this. In terms of her own prospects, it made little sense. She is an outsider. The storyteller keeps stressing 'the Moabite'. And widows in that society had no security or settled income. Their life together would have been hard.

Back in Bethlehem they need food, so Ruth goes gleaning. Boaz, the farmer, learns who she is, and of her generous and costly care for Naomi, a relative. He responds generously to her – and more than once.

The turning points in this story of vulnerability, loss and need all come about when someone does more than is necessary or required – when they respond generously. Those who do not are not blamed; they did no wrong. But neither are they part of the story of transformation. In acting generously, Ruth and Boaz are behaving like God, whose love and grace towards us always overflows what is strictly or sensibly 'necessary'. Think of all the leftovers after feeding the 5,000 or all that wine at Cana!

In our challenging times we can easily be more aware of our lack and of scarcity. The call to be generous can feel impractical and unaffordable. The generous response easily becomes unfamiliar. The book of Ruth tells us it actually changes everything.

Lord, may my words and responses be unnecessarily generous.

DAVID RUNCORN

Rizpah's voice

The king took the two sons of Rizpah… and the five sons of Merab [and] gave them into the hands of the Gibeonites… Then Rizpah the daughter of Aiah took sackcloth, and spread it on a rock for herself, from the beginning of harvest until rain fell on them from the heavens; she did not allow the birds of the air to come on the bodies by day, or the wild animals by night.

On a hilltop outside the town a woman is sitting in silence beside the bodies of her sons and their half-brothers. Rizpah is the widow of King Saul. The executions were the initiative of King David. Their lack of honourable burial was a further insult. There was no greater shame in the ancient world. Under a makeshift shelter, as famine wracks the land, Rizpah keeps vigil. Night and day, in heat and cold, she honours the dead. She drives away the vultures and the wild dogs. She watches and she waits. This very public wake is an act of extraordinary courage, honouring and defiance. We never hear her voice. She speaks through her actions.

This disturbing story is all too familiar around the world today. People still keep watch over loved ones. They keep vigil outside police stations and prisons, by military checkpoints, in makeshift graveyards. During the terrible oppression in Chile, the women would silently dance their protest outside the military headquarters, as if their loved ones were still in their arms. They would recognise Rizpah all too well. They know what held her there. In this way, at the risk of their lives, injustice becomes heard and seen.

Her actions shamed the powers that be. She called King David back to core values of compassion and justice. She reminded him, in so doing, that these qualities reflect the likeness of God too. She also reminds me of the women who waited and watched with Jesus by his cross. I suspect that God shared Rizpah's vigil on that hilltop.

King David learned of her actions and responded. Belatedly, he honoured the dead. Only then, we read, did God answer prayers for the land. The famine came to an end (2 Samuel 21:14). Rizpah calls out protest and injustice – and God hears and acts.

Lord, may I sit with the voiceless and oppressed.

DAVID RUNCORN

Curious faith

Moses… led his flock beyond the wilderness, and came to Horeb, the mountain of God. There the angel of the Lord appeared to him in a flame of fire out of a bush; he looked, and the bush was blazing, yet it was not consumed. Then Moses said, 'I must turn aside and look at this great sight, and see why the bush is not burned up.' When the Lord saw that he had turned aside to see, God called to him out of the bush, 'Moses, Moses!… Come no closer! Remove the sandals from your feet, for the place on which you are standing is holy ground.'

Picture a lone shepherd, in the searing heat of the wilderness, seeking grazing ground for the flock. The story suggests he has strayed beyond his usual territory. Out of the corner of his eye he sees a bush burning. That is not unusual. That terrain is tinder dry and it only takes the slightest spark to reduce everything to ash in minutes. But this bush goes on burning.

So it is that a story of liberation that has inspired nations and communities through history begins when a shepherd in the wilderness is curious enough to break his routine, turn aside and take a closer look at something unusual, unfamiliar. How many bushes Moses had missed before this one, we do not know. How many do we miss in the familiar routines of daily life?

God is never so revealed as to be obvious. He generally does not plant himself in front of us or force himself on our attention. The faith that grows and meets God is inquisitive. It goes exploring. It is adventurous, not content to stay on well-worn trails, and it is willing to be inconvenienced. Curiosity is a vital but neglected quality in the journey of faith.

Turning is the key movement in this story. It is in our discipleship too, from our baptism onwards – 'I *turn* to Christ.' Like Moses we must be willing to turn aside, break our routines, go wandering. We must risk arriving late, or not at all! But may our faith never be so settled on familiar paths that we miss what is trying to catch our attention – out there, in the corner of our eye.

Lord, provoke me into being more curious.

DAVID RUNCORN

The playful God

The Lord created me at the beginning of his work, the first of his acts of long ago. Ages ago I was set up, at the first, before the beginning of the earth… when he marked out the foundations of the earth, then I was beside him, like a master worker; and I was daily his delight, rejoicing before him always, rejoicing in his inhabited world and delighting in the human race.

Even the most faithful Bible translations can be incomplete. 'Master worker' here also carries a sense of 'intimate companion' or 'the apple of his eye'. 'Rejoicing' is more fully translated 'playing'. Delight, fun, joy, play and companionship are all there at the beginning of all things. The image could be a child playing in the divine workshop.

In a church in Northamptonshire is a sculpture of Mary and Jesus. Most depictions of the holy family are serious and freighted with deep spiritual symbolism. But in this sculpture, they are playing. Just having fun. I almost hear them laughing out loud. Why is this such an unfamiliar voice?

Wisdom, in Proverbs, is God's creating life at work and it seems to be exhilarating fun! Also notice that Wisdom's endless, playful delight is in this created world, in 'the human race' – in you and me. We give God delight and joy. He finds us fun to be with. Can you imagine that?

The 13th-century Christian mystic Mechthild of Magdeburg heard God saying to her, 'I, God, am your playmate! I will lead the child in you in wonderful ways, for I have chosen you.' Did not Jesus tell us that we must become like children to enter his life? He often likened himself to the image of wisdom. He once complained to his own over-serious generation, 'We played… and you did not dance' (Matthew 11:17). There is nothing trivial about this invitation. Play can often be a very serious activity. But seriousness often struggles to be playful at all.

Can you imagine yourself caught up in the hands of Wisdom – just playing and laughing together, delighting in the creative life of God, as it endlessly renews all things? Playful wisdom is calling. It is too often an unfamiliar voice.

Lord, I want to play in your life and love.

DAVID RUNCORN

Chasing the wind

Vanity of vanities, says the Teacher, vanity of vanities! All is vanity. What do people gain from all the toil at which they toil under the sun?... I, the Teacher, when king over Israel in Jerusalem, applied my mind to seek and to search out by wisdom all that is done under heaven; it is an unhappy business that God has given to human beings to be busy with. I saw all the deeds that are done under the sun; and see, all is vanity and a chasing after wind.

Ecclesiastes is not a comfortable book. With the exception of a few familiar verses, we tend to leave much of it unread. 'The Teacher', as he is called, easily sounds simply depressed to our ears. Has he lost faith? Or is this, rather, an unfamiliar voice of faith that we need to listen to?

The repeated refrain 'All is vanity' is well known, though it is easily misunderstood. He is not saying life is meaningless. This is not the voice of despair. The Hebrew word, *hevel*, means 'vapour' or 'breath'. Life is gossamer thin, light as breath, passing as the morning mist. In the light of that, how are we to live? Given such a precious and fragile gift as this life, it is vital to ask the right questions of it. 'What do people gain... what is the point... what is its value?' the Teacher asks. No questions demand more care and attention.

Once we confess how light and ephemeral our lives are, we may better recognise the folly in what we can spend our time seeking and doing. As Ellen Davis once prayed, 'Life is so short. Let me not live it stupidly.'

The Teacher's voice is unsentimental, raw and honest. He would not be relaxing company at a dinner party. Perhaps that is why we need him. His wisdom is hard won. Clearly some of what he has given his life to has left him empty and searching. All is *hevel*. But rather than this being the voice of a world weary, even cynical, philosopher, Ecclesiastes is better understood as an extended plea for God's mercy.

God, help me turn from illusions to the life that is truly your gift.

DAVID RUNCORN

Honest voices

Remove your stroke from me; I am worn down by the blows of your hand. You chastise mortals in punishment for sin, consuming like a moth what is dear to them; surely everyone is a mere breath. Hear my prayer, O Lord, and give ear to my cry; do not hold your peace at my tears. For I am your passing guest, an alien, like all my forebears. Turn your gaze away from me, that I may smile again, before I depart and am no more.

Have you known times when the demands of life and faith can become too much? We simply cannot do it anymore. Believing is a burden rather than a joy. And, for whatever the reason, God is part of the problem, not the answer. Teresa of Ávila once famously prayed to Jesus, 'If this is how you treat your friends, it is no wonder you have so few!'

During a time of personal struggle, I remember friends praying that God would be *more* real and *nearer* to me. It was lovingly intended but exactly what I *didn't* want in that moment. I needed God to give me some space. But I didn't know how to tell them, or God.

The voice of this psalmist is unfamiliar to our faith and praying it may be hard because we believe it is not acceptable. But these painful verses remind us that God does not require us to be polite before him. It serves no purpose. God can take it. He knows it all anyway.

This psalm reminds us that our rawest pain and perplexity does not need to be hidden from our prayers. I recall someone once said that 'feelings do not decompose if you bury them'. Holding lids on struggles of which we feel ashamed simply adds to the burden. So let us be honest. If we are exhausted, we need to rest. There are times we must let others bear what we, for a time, cannot. These may be times to seek help to understand what is going on and why. We may be misunderstanding what God is asking of us.

If this is where our prayers must start from, let it be so. The psalmist understood this well.

Lord, help me to pray with honesty.

DAVID RUNCORN

The talking donkey

When the donkey saw the angel of the Lord, it lay down under Balaam, and he was angry and beat it with his staff. Then the Lord opened the donkey's mouth, and it said to Balaam, 'What have I done to you to make you beat me these three times?'… Then the Lord opened Balaam's eyes, and he saw the angel of the Lord standing in the road with his sword drawn. So he bowed low and fell face down.

The Israelites were spreading across the land. The surrounding nations were fearful. Balaam was one of their prophets. You commissioned people like him to negotiate with the gods for your particular needs or problems. King Balak books Balaam to curse the Israelites, and so destroy them. But when Balaam seeks discernment, Israel's God (the true God) turns up and gives him an unambiguous blessing for Israel.

What follows is very funny in a cartoonish way. It has been said that there are three asses in this story: the king, who thought he could buy divine power for his own gain; Balaam, who received very clear guidance from God but kept changing his mind; and his donkey, the only one in the story who sees what is actually going on and knows what he has to do!

This story contains several unfamiliar voices. One is Balaam's: a foreign sage through whom God speaks an unexpected blessing to his people. The other is the donkey that speaks. In the Bible, wisdom surfaces in unlikely places and with unlikely people (or creatures). Those thought wise can be exposed as foolish, and those dismissed as foolish or unimportant become a voice of divine revelation. God is found working through complete outsiders, even those who might be expected to oppose his ways. God can and does speak through anyone or anything to reveal his purposes.

What is the challenge of hearing a donkey speak? Perhaps it is to trust that God is working and speaking through all of life and not just in narrowly religious ways. We are to be open to hearing God speaking among the least, the unexpected and the 'outsiders', and to follow.

Lord, help me to listen to the voices of your donkeys.

DAVID RUNCORN

The voice of the wise

Joab's forces came... battering the wall to break it down. Then a wise woman called from the city, 'Listen! Listen!... Come here, I want to speak to you.' He came near her; and the woman said, 'Are you Joab?' He answered, 'I am.' Then she said to him, 'Listen to the words of your servant.' He answered, 'I am listening.' Then she said, 'They used to say in the old days, "Let them inquire at Abel"; and so they would settle a matter. I am one of those who are peaceable and faithful in Israel; you seek to destroy a city that is a mother in Israel; why will you swallow up the heritage of the Lord?'

This story comes in the lowest moment of King David's reign. The nation is violently divided. Joab is David's brutal enforcer. The walled town of Abel of Beth-maacah suddenly finds itself on the front line of the conflict when a rebel leader takes refuge there. Without word or warning, Joab's troops arrive and start battering down the walls. Soon all shall be slaughtered, the town destroyed. Frighteningly similar scenes occur in the world today.

But someone appears on the walls. With remarkable courage, and at risk of her life, an unnamed woman calls to Joab. Remember the significance of first words in Hebrew storytelling (see Tuesday 20 September)? Her first words are 'Listen! Listen!' She tells Joab that she and her community are peacemakers. People have always gone to this town for wisdom on issues. She calls Joab (and King David) to 'listen'. The hammering falls silent.

Until we become listeners, many voices will be unfamiliar. Whenever we are unwilling or unable to make space for the possibility of other views and to take time to listen to them, our encounters quickly become battering experiences. Exchanges on social media are too often an example of this. In social, political and church life, we urgently need to recover the lost art of listening to different voices and convictions, instead of tearing them down. Relationships, community, trust, respect and mutual understanding are impossible without listening.

Now, as then, may we be known as listeners and so become peacemakers in our own conflicted times.

Lord, help me to be a listener, and so make peace.

DAVID RUNCORN

The voice of love

My beloved speaks and says to me: 'Arise, my love, my fair one, and come away; for now the winter is past, the rain is over and gone. The flowers appear on the earth; the time of singing has come, and the voice of the turtle-dove is heard in our land… My beloved is mine and I am his… Until the day breathes and the shadows flee, turn, my beloved, be like a gazelle or a young stag on the cleft mountains.'

In the middle of the ancient Hebrew scriptures is a short, erotic love poem. Some think it should be left unfamiliar! But there it is, an utterly exuberant, unembarrassed celebration of human love and desire that more often leaves us fearful of its power. What does this Song sing to us today?

First, without inhibition, the Song celebrates the human longing for intimate, harmonious, enduring relationships with another. Without ever being casual or indulgent, it celebrates the incomparable joy of faithful, sexual relationship and the delights of committed desire and expression.

Second, the Song affirms that human intimacy finds its fullest meaning in a deeper union with divine love: with God. The relationship of the spiritual and the sexual is wholly positive. The Song holds together what is too often kept apart.

Third, the Song is set in a garden. A garden is where it all began and then went horribly wrong. Yet here all is fruitful, pungent with blossom and full of life. All that was lost is here found restored. The couple embrace in unashamed delight. The poetic imagery also expresses divine union, worship and adoration. The sheer vibrancy of surrounding creation is a theme throughout the poem. When human desire and love find full expression – in each other and in God – creation itself returns to being the garden of God's gift, presence and delight.

The original threefold rupture is healed: humanity with each other; humanity and God; humanity and nature. The Song invites us to come with unfamiliar joy and hope to something God-given which lies at the heart of being human, but which too easily leaves us anxious and fearful. The time of singing has come.

Lord teach me how to sing this song.

DAVID RUNCORN

Holy Habits: Fellowship

I find that the word 'fellowship' is inclined to create a kind of spiritual indigestion in me. To my ear, it has an out-of-date feel to it. I trip up on the fact that it is not exactly an inclusive word, with *fellow* as its root. It also has a habit of transporting me back to my early Christian days, where 'fellowship' meant gathering together with rather over-eager and intense Christians who wanted to look and behave as differently as possible to the secular world around them. I find it can also conjure up the typical caricature of damp church halls and lukewarm tea. Generally, I try to find a substitute word.

But there comes the problem. What word? 'Community' is the most obvious substitute, but that is a word that is used for such a wide range of human groups, that, without further definition, it is almost meaningless.

So in the end I go back to 'fellowship'. The *Oxford English Dictionary* defines it as 'a group of people meeting to pursue a shared interest or aim,' and, for me, this does a reasonably good job of defining the word as I see it used in our Bible. The group in this case is the followers of Christ, seeking to serve his kingdom.

In these coming two weeks we shall be exploring the scriptures to ascertain just what kind of community God desires to see among the human beings who have chosen to follow him. We shall see that from the first pages of Genesis to the end of Revelation, there is a consistent message that God is profoundly interested in human relationships, and that humans are at their best when they work in a creative harmony with others.

Sadly, the scriptures are also full of stories of pain and tragedy caused by the breakdown of relationships. In the New Testament, 'fellowship' is usually used to translate the Greek word *koinonia*. This is a feminine noun chosen by the New Testament writers, and it describes a particularly strong bond of love and trust between humans. We may not succeed in finding a better translation than 'fellowship'. But the word is not important; living in the reality of its meaning is.

MICHAEL MITTON

It is not good for humans to be alone

Then the Lord God said, 'It is not good that the man should be alone; I will make him a helper as his partner.' So out of the ground the Lord God formed every animal of the field and every bird of the air, and brought them to the man to see what he would call them; and whatever the man called each living creature, that was its name. The man gave names to all cattle, and to the birds of the air, and to every animal of the field; but for the man there was not found a helper as his partner.

This account of creation in Genesis presents a beautiful image of God. He is tender and intimate, so close to the man that he breathes life into his nostrils (Genesis 2:7). He plants a garden for him that not only provides sustenance for the man, but nourishes his spirit through its beauty (v. 9). By the time you get to verse 18, you have the impression that God loves seeing the man delighting in this fresh, beautiful and sustaining creation.

But he notices a problem: the man is lonely. God's first attempt at curing the man's loneliness is sending animals and birds. It is clear they are not enough. It is then that God realises just what the man needs: a woman. So he forms this human from the ribcage of the man – the bone nearest to his heart.

The message is clear: humans were designed to be close to their creator *and* close to each other. But the next chapter of this story is of the fall, where the intimacy between the man and the woman and between the humans and their creator is dreadfully fractured.

Humans have developed into a multitude of different personalities with varying degrees of need for human companionship. But what this story from Genesis tells us is that the need for meaningful relationships is one of our most basic.

Thank God today for the relationships that are significant for you.

MICHAEL MITTON

The Babel disaster

Now the whole earth had one language and the same words. And as they migrated from the east, they came upon a plain in the land of Shinar and settled there. And they said to one another, 'Come, let us make bricks, and burn them thoroughly.' And they had brick for stone, and bitumen for mortar. Then they said, 'Come, let us build ourselves a city, and a tower with its top in the heavens, and let us make a name for ourselves; otherwise we shall be scattered abroad upon the face of the whole earth.'

The story begins with a world that is united by one language until a particular group decides it wants to be one up on the others by building a huge ziggurat. They feel this will ensure they can be self-reliant and will gain fame in the world. They want to be seen as the best. And it will ensure they will not be scattered. But the writer knows they are foolish, not least because the building materials they use are not strong enough for a great building. They are also foolish because they make no reference to God.

The story then switches to heaven, where we have another group conversation (vv. 5–7). This is the heavenly community, who are concerned about the humans. They can see that this plan is all about using human devices to secure power in this world. So God comes 'down' (v. 5). Their high tower is still tiny compared to God's heaven.

God does the very thing they dread: he confuses their language so they can no longer understand each other. They could have given time to learning each other's languages, but instead, they head off to different parts of the world forming their own tribes of like-minded people speaking their own language.

This story has been used to explain the multitude of languages in this world. But it also contains a profound insight about human nature: that searching for power in this world has a damaging effect on our relationships. Also, building community on earth without any reference to the community of heaven spells trouble. Heaven and earth were always meant to work closely together.

How do you understand the community of heaven?

MICHAEL MITTON

The community of blessing

Now the Lord said to Abram, 'Go from your country and your kindred and your father's house to the land that I will show you. I will make of you a great nation, and I will bless you, and make your name great, so that you will be a blessing. I will bless those who bless you, and the one who curses you I will curse; and in you all the families of the earth shall be blessed.'

After the despair of the Babel story, we move on to a story of immense hope. It is the story of Abram, and it is another story about community. At first, it seems anything but. Abram has to abandon his home community and his homeland and head off on a pilgrimage with no clear destination. Unlike the people of Babel, Abram desires to do what God wants, even if that means breaking ties with his home. Right at the heart of this call is the promise of a new community. It is not an exclusive community, for it is a community that will be mindful of all the families of the earth. This community is for the blessing of all families. This is a community that can heal the brokenness of Babel.

We know only too well through our reading of the scriptures that the outworking of this plan was not simple. Abraham (as he becomes), though wonderfully faithful, is also far from perfect, and the generations that follow him fail time and time again. Much of the Old Testament describes the very mixed fortunes of this nation of God, who are supposed to be blessing every family on earth. Too often human pride and the ignoring of God's ways lead to more broken community.

When Matthew came to write his gospel, he started it by giving a genealogy of Jesus 'the son of David, the son of Abraham' (Matthew 1:1). He reminds his readers of the generations from Abraham. The promise is still there – God desires to build a community that will bless the world. His gospel is all about how, with Jesus, there is real hope that this community of faith and blessing can be established.

How do you think a community of faith can bless 'the families of the earth'?

MICHAEL MITTON

Life together

How very good and pleasant it is when kindred live together in unity! It is like the precious oil on the head, running down upon the beard, on the beard of Aaron, running down over the collar of his robes. It is like the dew of Hermon, which falls on the mountains of Zion. For there the Lord ordained his blessing, life forevermore.

Before we leave the Old Testament, we take a look at a psalm on the theme of fellowship. Psalm 133 simply wants to celebrate the power of human community. It is a psalm designed to bring people back to their senses. It feels like it is saying, 'Stop your bickering and remember the power of unity.' It picks up the image of anointing oil on Aaron, an anointing marked by abundance. It is saying that there is a rich flow of blessing that comes from unity. It also uses the image of the dew of Mount Hermon. The little drops of dew refresh the great mountain, and contribute to the making of flowing rivers. So, says the psalmist, don't despise the little acts of community, because they can have huge consequences.

Dietrich Bonhoeffer quotes this psalm at the beginning of *Life Together*. Bonhoeffer led a seminary of the German 'Confessing Church' just prior to World War II, and his book came out of his experience of living in community. One of the insights he gained from this experience was to do with aloneness. He wrote, 'Only in the fellowship do we learn to be rightly alone and only in aloneness do we learn to live rightly in the fellowship… Let the one who cannot be alone beware of community. Let the one who is not in community beware of being alone.'

Bonhoeffer tells us that there is a right aloneness in fellowship. What does he mean? Maybe he is thinking that it is in the company of others that our unique self can flourish. And he also suggests that when we are on our own, we can stand back and reflect on how we can flourish and help others to flourish in the fellowship.

What do you think Bonhoeffer means? What is God saying to you through his words?

MICHAEL MITTON

A commandment in the night

After receiving the piece of bread, [Judas] immediately went out. And it was night. When he had gone out, Jesus said… 'Little children, I am with you only a little longer. You will look for me; and as I said to the Jews so now I say to you, "Where I am going, you cannot come." I give you a new commandment, that you love one another. Just as I have loved you, you also should love one another. By this everyone will know that you are my disciples, if you have love for one another.'

In this story, John introduces us to the terrible act of betrayal that is being planned by Judas. John tells us that 'it was night', and you get the feeling he is telling us this because Judas' betrayal has triggered the process that will lead to the darkness of Jesus' death. Jesus is clearly aware of what is happening. Yet from this dark place, we have words from Jesus that have the power to radiate light into the darkest place: he delivers his new commandment.

Jesus says to his disciples, 'You should now love each other in exactly the same way as I have been loving you.' He adds that when they do, people will recognise that they are his disciples. Quite what they made of this commandment is hard to know. Probably most of them felt they could do a lot better when it came to loving the other disciples. Later they would discover the extent to which Jesus loved each and every one of them, including Judas. This was no superficial, feelings-driven love. It was an extraordinary and radical act of love that cost Jesus his life.

For the first couple of hundred years, Christians did not do too badly at following this commandment. In AD200, the Christian teacher Tertullian told of how the pagans would remark, 'Look how the Christians love one another.' We feel a sense of shame that as the years have gone by, such an observation from those outside the church is far too rare. But any talk of fellowship has to reckon with this commandment delivered by Jesus in the dark of night.

What is God saying to you today through this commandment?

MICHAEL MITTON

Kindred spirits

While he was still speaking to the crowds, his mother and his brothers were standing outside, wanting to speak to him. Someone told him, 'Look, your mother and your brothers are standing outside, wanting to speak to you.' But to the one who had told him this, Jesus replied, 'Who is my mother, and who are my brothers?' And pointing to his disciples, he said, 'Here are my mother and my brothers! For whoever does the will of my Father in heaven is my brother and sister and mother.'

It is hard to read this story without feeling that Jesus was being a little harsh on his mother and family, not to say, rude. The story clearly held importance for Matthew, Mark and Luke, because they all report it in their gospels. You could conclude that Jesus is effectively saying that he has now moved on from his nuclear family, and he has got more important things to be doing. But this is not consistent with his treatment of Mary at the cross, where he clearly held a great love and concern for her (see John 19:26–27).

As I read it, this is a story not so much about a rejection of Jesus' domestic family, but more a statement by him about the nature of relationships among the disciples. Jesus is saying that anyone who decides to do the will of their Father in heaven is taken into a new family group. Consequently, Jesus is as close to a disciple as he is to his own mother or sibling. Rather than belittling his immediate family, he is honouring all who count themselves as children of their heavenly Father.

We all have mixed experiences of families, but whatever we may feel about this image of the Christian community being a family, it does tell us that Jesus expected us to relate to one another as if we are connected by blood ties. This brings responsibility and hope: responsibility to steward well our relationships with others in the fellowship; hope that when relationships get tough, the blood that ties us is Christ's.

What is your instinctive feeling about seeing the fellowship as family?
How might the cross of Christ be a resource for healing when there are
problems in the family?

MICHAEL MITTON

Keep it simple

One of the scribes came near and heard them disputing with one another, and seeing that he answered them well, he asked him, 'Which commandment is the first of all?' Jesus answered, 'The first is, "Hear, O Israel: the Lord our God, the Lord is one; you shall love the Lord your God with all your heart, and with all your soul, and with all your mind, and with all your strength." The second is this, "You shall love your neighbour as yourself." There is no other commandment greater than these.'

The scribes' job was to interpret the law in all its many rules and regulations, both the written law in the scriptures and the complex world of the oral law. As they saw it, it was the law that bound the community together. While the scribes were known for their attention to minutiae, they also liked to summarise complex issues into one sentence. This particular scribe is clearly impressed by Jesus, so he asks him to say which is the best commandment.

Jesus answers that there are two: love God and love people. Out of all the many laws in the Torah and the multitude of petty laws in the oral tradition of the day, Jesus says that these two commandments stand head and shoulders above the others. In Matthew's version of this story, he adds that the whole of the law and prophets hang on these two commandments (Matthew 22:40). The scribe is quite satisfied with this reply, and Jesus commends him as one who is not far from the kingdom of God (v. 34).

The call of a Christian is really very simple: love God and love people. This is the core of our fellowship and mission. Even if you can't make head nor tail of some parts of the creed, you can get this. You may find yourself baffled by difficult ethical issues, but you can still understand these two commandments. All through the ages Christians have been scribe-like in creating highly complex religious rules about beliefs and behaviours. But Jesus kept it simple. And yet it is these two simple commandments that we find so challenging and so hard to keep.

How can you love God and love people today?

MICHAEL MITTON

The outrageous commandment

'You have heard that it was said, "You shall love your neighbour and hate your enemy." But I say to you, Love your enemies and pray for those who persecute you, so that you may be children of your Father in heaven; for he makes his sun rise on the evil and on the good, and sends rain on the righteous and on the unrighteous. For if you love those who love you, what reward do you have?'

The disciples would have nodded in agreement at Jesus summarising the commandments into those of loving God and loving neighbour. Being kind and doing good to the people around you were values they had grown up with. This was a reasonable command. However, in today's reading, Jesus stretches this love command to a disturbing extreme: love your enemy. The disciples would have seen this as highly unreasonable. Love the Romans with all their cruelty? Love the tax-gatherers with their thieving ways? Love the Pharisees with the massive burdens they placed on the people? 'Come on, Jesus,' they might have said. 'Be reasonable.'

I am told that the command to love the enemy is unique to Christianity. It is utterly radical and contrary to human nature and seems quite unreasonable. But for the followers of the Christ of the cross, it is fundamental to our religion.

So who is the enemy? The enemy is anyone who threatens me, and if that is the case then the enemy may well be in my fellowship. It is anyone whose behaviour, beliefs or attitudes challenges and disturbs me. It is the person I try to avoid. And this makes them the person I am called to love. This is where the gospel gets tough, because we all know how hard it is to love people who annoy and threaten us. Churches are frequently torn apart by strife, where people conveniently ignore this command of Jesus. Yet where people have dared to live according to this command, they have frequently found the Holy Spirit at work with gifts of healing and reconciliation. This command is not an idle aspiration; it has the power to transform us. It is one of the unique qualities of Christian fellowship.

Who is your 'enemy'? How can you love them?

MICHAEL MITTON

Babel healed

Amazed and astonished, they asked, 'Are not all these who are speaking Galileans? And how is it that we hear, each of us, in our own native language? Parthians, Medes, Elamites, and residents of Mesopotamia, Judea and Cappadocia, Pontus and Asia, Phrygia and Pamphylia, Egypt and the parts of Libya belonging to Cyrene, and visitors from Rome, both Jews and proselytes, Cretans and Arabs – in our own languages we hear them speaking about God's deeds of power'… They devoted themselves to the apostles' teaching and fellowship, to the breaking of bread and the prayers.

Last week we read the sad story of the tower of Babel, where people were divided by a multitude of different languages. Here in this Pentecost story, the reverse happens. People of different languages are united in a quite extraordinary way. Galileans were not noted as being highly educated people with a knack for mastering several foreign languages. Yet here in a busy street in Jerusalem, a Parthian is hearing one Galilean disciple speaking fluent Parthian and an Egyptian hears another singing to her in perfect Egyptian. The disciples have been given a supernatural ability to speak another language without doing any evening classes. Many of us feel a distinct envy at this fast track to language acquisition! No wonder these foreigners are amazed and astonished. Luke tells us that around 3,000 people are added to their number that day. These presumably include people from the various language groups, and some of these stay on in Jerusalem and become those who are part of the new fellowship of the followers of Christ.

What became clear that Pentecost day was that the message of this Spirit-inspired kingdom of God was not only relevant to all cultures, but there was a power at work that transcended the usual suspicions and misgivings of one culture to another, healing the divides and drawing humans into a new multi-ethnic community. Such diversity was part of the original DNA of the church. Whether the original disciples continued to be given these languages, we don't know. But one way or another these multi-ethnic groups flourished in the days when this infant church was so alive.

What does this Pentecost story say to you about the diversity of fellowship?

MICHAEL MITTON

So this is what fellowship means

Awe came upon everyone, because many wonders and signs were being done by the apostles. All who believed were together and had all things in common; they would sell their possessions and goods and distribute the proceeds to all, as any had need. Day by day, as they spent much time together in the temple, they broke bread at home and ate their food with glad and generous hearts, praising God and having the goodwill of all the people. And day by day the Lord added to their number those who were being saved.

A direct result of Pentecost is community. These disparate people are thrown together, and Luke tells us that there were several dynamic characteristics of this new community of the followers of Jesus.

It was a community in which *miracles* took place. This had been a significant part of Jesus' ministry, and now it was being carried on by the apostles whom Jesus had trained. It was a community that enjoyed a high degree of *sharing*, particularly of possessions. A direct effect of the Spirit seems to have been that people now had a light touch on the things they possessed. Things were far less important. It was a community that had a special concern for the *poor*. They have a sensitivity to the people around them who are suffering poverty. So they raise money from selling possessions, and giving the money away. It was a community that loved to *worship*. They go to the temple, the formal place of worship. But they also enjoy more informal worship in each other's homes. As most homes were not large, these would have been small groups. It was a community that was *respected* by the local community. They were seen to be a good influence for the city. It was a community that was constantly *growing*. It was *generous* and *welcoming*, and not inward-looking.

We cannot but feel admiration and delight at these qualities found in this early church. It was surely exactly the kind of community Jesus had trained his disciples to build. And it is surely the kind of community he still desires to see today.

Which of these characteristics stands out for you today?
How can you help grow them in your fellowship?

MICHAEL MITTON

Primal divisions healed

For in Christ Jesus you are all children of God through faith. As many of you as were baptised into Christ have clothed yourselves with Christ. There is no longer Jew or Greek, there is no longer slave or free, there is no longer male and female; for all of you are one in Christ Jesus. And if you belong to Christ, then you are Abraham's offspring, heirs according to the promise.

In his letter to the Galatians, Paul is having to defend the very open form of fellowship that was experienced at Pentecost. As time went on, some Jewish believers felt indignant that Gentile converts to Christianity were not undergoing the requirements of the Jewish law, such as circumcision. They saw Jewish Christians as superior to Gentile Christians. This was anathema to Paul, who profoundly believed that the gospel was free to all. But he would have well understood these Judaisers (as they were called). For Paul himself had been a very devout Jew and would have used a prayer popular at the time, thanking God that 'Thou hast not made me a Gentile, a slave or a woman.'

But Paul's teaching in our passage today was most likely not just a throwaway sentiment to counter an old prayer. It may well be that he had pondered the divisions that caused such suffering in the world. Maybe he identified three that were primal divisions: 'Jew or Greek' speaks of the great divides between tribal cultures, the divide that was so beautifully healed at Pentecost; 'slave or free' speaks of the terrible economic divides, where those living in extravagant wealth oppress those who are poor; 'male and female' speaks of the gender divide that has caused arguably more pain even than the other two.

For Paul, the Christian community was one in which these three dreadful divides were healed through the work of Christ. If you belong to Christ, then you will no longer tolerate such divides. It is sad to reflect that nearly 2,000 years after Paul, these divides still exist, even in the church. Paul would remind us that we are here to build a fellowship that models a healed world.

How might God call you to help heal these divisions?

MICHAEL MITTON

Threats to fellowship

Now I appeal to you, brothers and sisters, by the name of our Lord Jesus Christ, that all of you should be in agreement and that there should be no divisions among you, but that you should be united in the same mind and the same purpose. For it has been reported to me by Chloe's people that there are quarrels among you, my brothers and sisters. What I mean is that each of you says, 'I belong to Paul', or 'I belong to Apollos', or 'I belong to Cephas', or 'I belong to Christ.'

I think any of us would have forgiven Paul if occasionally he felt like giving up. Take Corinth, for example. He arrived there around AD50 and founded a church. He invested time and energy into the leadership, then went off to Ephesus to plant a church there, keeping in touch with Corinth through letters. However, soon after he left the city, some people he calls 'super-apostles' arrive (2 Corinthians 11:5). They are full of complaints about Paul, and they challenge his leadership and authority. The result of this is chaos in Corinth and hence the Corinthian correspondence. Paul had to write his letters because the happy church that he planted was being damaged by divisiveness driven by people who thought they knew a good deal more about God than Paul did.

Paul was facing a problem that has expressed itself in one form or another throughout the history of the church: Christians thinking that they know better than other Christians and then setting up camps that support their way of thinking. Paul's response is to provide as clear teaching as he can. But he also uses a most unusual method: vulnerability. This is expressed most beautifully in 2 Corinthians 12:1–10, his moving account of his vision of the 'third heaven' and the revelation that God's strength is made perfect in human weakness and that grace is all that is needed. Paul's way of healing divisions in the fellowship is not by exercising power and asserting authority, but by acknowledging his weakness. When we experience the grace of God, power games in church appear foolish and pointless.

How can you be an agent of the grace of God in your church?

MICHAEL MITTON

Love is the only option

There is no fear in love, but perfect love casts out fear; for fear has to do with punishment, and whoever fears has not reached perfection in love. We love because he first loved us. Those who say, 'I love God', and hate their brothers or sisters, are liars; for those who do not love a brother or sister whom they have seen, cannot love God whom they have not seen. The commandment we have from him is this: those who love God must love their brothers and sisters also.

The message of John's first letter is essentially that God is light and that loving one another is not optional but essential. It is generally reckoned that he writes his letter just before the end of the first century, so the church has been going for several decades. During that time, alongside the wonderful bursts of gospel light happening all over the Roman empire, there are also some dark shadows. There are those who want to obscure the light by promoting ideas that deceive and confuse the new believers. There are also those who find the whole business of loving far too difficult and therefore try to neatly bypass Jesus' command to love one another.

So John comes in with his wisdom and warm heart and addresses all this. He has clearly thought much about love during his long life. He notices how humans are all too often driven by fear: fear of failure, of others, of losing face and of losing power, to name but a few. He is seeing signs of churches being dominated by people who are more driven by fear than love. There are people who claim to love God greatly, but when John looks at the way they treat others, he sees no sign of love in their hearts. John makes it completely clear: loving God means loving the humans he created. That's the deal. If you love God, but don't love people, you are a hypocrite.

Nowhere in the scriptures does it say that loving people is easy. But John says it starts with allowing ourselves to be loved. True fellowship happens among those who have learned what it means to live as the beloved of God.

How might you grow in love?

MICHAEL MITTON

Home

Then I saw a new heaven and a new earth; for the first heaven and the first earth had passed away, and the sea was no more. And I saw the holy city, the new Jerusalem, coming down out of heaven from God, prepared as a bride adorned for her husband. And I heard a loud voice from the throne saying, 'See, the home of God is among mortals. He will dwell with them; they will be his peoples, and God himself will be with them.'

On the island of Patmos, John is busy writing to several churches who are under his care. No doubt, there are times when he is preoccupied with matters of church governance and sorting out problems when people disagree with each other. Then one day, the heavens open and he sees things he never imagined seeing. Glimpses of the future break into the present and he scratches down on his parchment what he sees and hears. His record is packed full of mysterious images, codes, numbers and much that baffles us.

But within all this, there are some wonderfully lucid pieces, such as today's passage. This is probably the best-known section of his book, and it never fails to touch me. John actually catches sight of a heaven and an earth that are utterly new and are replacing the old ones. One would then expect that all this world will be gathered up and taken into heaven. But, no. This new Jerusalem, inhabited by God, is planted on earth. It will be a home where humans have finally learned how to live well together.

Amid the beautiful messages in this image comes the discovery that God views this world as his home. Once again God can walk with his humans in the garden in the cool of the day. In this world of the future, we shall enjoy perfect fellowship with God and with one another. John did not write his book just to tantalise his readers. For him, the vision of the future was given to encourage Christ's followers in the present. Proper meditation on the home of God in the future evokes longing in us, and it inspires us to build such homes today.

How does John's vision touch you?

MICHAEL MITTON

On a journey

The spiritual life is often explored through the metaphor of a journey, and indeed every life is a journey – a journey into the unknown, sometimes overshadowed by pain and grief, sometimes illuminated by shafts of joy, but always full of surprises. During the next two weeks, however, we will be making a very real journey, with Paul and his companions, on the way to Jerusalem. While this journey is both historical and physical, it is also a spiritual journey, confronting Paul with unexpected challenges, trials and an intensive encounter with God's grace.

There are clear parallels between Paul's experience and some aspects of Jesus' own journey to Jerusalem. Jesus also sets off in faith as he embarks on what will be his final, agonising journey on earth. Both are warned repeatedly of the dangers of going to Jerusalem and the perils that await them there. Both choose to stay true to where they believe God is calling them to be, whatever it may cost. Both rebuke those who try to undermine their resolve. And both entrust themselves entirely to God's leading.

Like many millions of pilgrims through the ages, Paul begins his journey with a prayer. I have always been moved, particularly when travelling in Ireland, to see how travellers frequently embark on even the briefest of journeys by explicitly asking for God's blessing on the way ahead.

While Paul's journey reflects aspects of Jesus' journey, it also sheds light on our own life's pathways. For us, too, there will be hardships and injustices along the way, just as Paul had to face the cruelty and false accusations of his enemies. But there will also be consolations, like the loyal friend who stays with us through it all and speaks up for us when others are against us. And above all, there will be the constant presence of God, occasionally piercing the clouds in a shaft of healing, warming, life-restoring light. We too have our 'road to Damascus' moments that have, sometimes suddenly and unexpectedly but often more gently and gradually, turned our imagined human vision and power into blindness and helplessness, only to birth new insight from our floundering darkness, and a personal and undeniable certainty of God's continuous presence in our lives, whatever the future journey may hold.

MARGARET SILF

Setting sail

We came by a straight course to Cos, and the next day to Rhodes, and from there to Patara… We looked up the disciples and stayed [in Tyre] for seven days. Through the Spirit they told Paul not to go on to Jerusalem. When our days there were ended, we left and proceeded on our journey… We knelt down on the beach and prayed and said farewell to one another. Then we went on board the ship.

The pattern of Paul's journey begins, as perhaps your own life journey began, with a period of plain sailing, during which everything seems to be going to plan. The travellers pass without problems from one port to the next. But life rarely proceeds smoothly, and the calm is soon to be shattered. Paul is abruptly confronted by a stern warning against going to Jerusalem. Suddenly the journey resembles not so much one we might have taken ourselves, but one which Jesus actually did take. It recalls how Jesus too was warned, by Peter (Matthew 16:21–22), not to go to Jerusalem.

Yet both Jesus and Paul choose to go against this advice. 'Going to Jerusalem' for both of them means living true to what they believe God is asking them to do, whatever that might cost. This is much more than a journey. This is a mission which will cost them their lives.

Perhaps you have also experienced the disruption and upheaval caused when your plans are suddenly interrupted and called into question. Few of us travel far without encountering such barriers and obstacles. And perhaps you have also had to choose between a course of action that you know in your heart to be right and other more attractive and safer options.

Recognising the sacred nature of the forthcoming journey, Paul kneels on the beach to pray before departing. Irish readers especially may be reminded of St Brendan, who famously knelt on the beach before leaving his native land to embark on a life-changing voyage, entrusting himself entirely to God for all that lay ahead, leaving only his knee-prints in the sand.

Every life is a hazardous, but also a sacred, journey. May we have the grace to entrust our lives entirely to God's guiding, as we embark on each new day.

MARGARET SILF

Warning voices

While we were staying [in Caesarea] for several days, a prophet named Agabus came down from Judea. He came to us and took Paul's belt, bound his own hands and feet with it, and said, 'Thus says the Holy Spirit, "This is the way the Jews in Jerusalem will bind the man who owns this belt and will hand him over to the Gentiles."'

Today the warning against going to Jerusalem is delivered by the prophet Agabus, this time not merely in words, but also through a dramatic demonstration of the likely consequences of proceeding with the journey. Every teacher knows from experience the wisdom of the words, 'Tell me, and I forget. Show me, and I remember.' Agabus' actions speak louder than the earlier words of warning. As this scene unfolds, we can almost hear Jesus' own words to Peter, echoing down from the resurrection appearance in Galilee: 'When you grow old… someone else will fasten a belt around you and take you where you do not wish to go' (John 21:18).

Agabus' warning, however, though sincere and well-intentioned, stems from the natural human instinct to fear what threatens us and to avoid potential conflict. Both Paul and Jesus face dire consequences if they persist in going where they believe God is calling them. Our human condition programmes us to shun everything that threatens our survival. God's dream for humanity, however, is rooted in love, not fear, and love calls us to places where fear dare not tread.

The parallels between Paul's journey and the road that Jesus trod before him are becoming more and more apparent. A pattern is developing. Paul's plans and intentions are repeatedly challenged by warnings that are stark and uncompromising. Jesus too travelled from place to place, supported by the kindness of friends. Jesus too was warned of what lay ahead for him in Jerusalem. Both struggle with their fears, but both choose the course that love is asking of them.

The cost of discipleship is high. How will Paul proceed? How will *we* proceed?

The voices warning us of the risks of discipleship can be loud and insistent, but the quiet promptings of the Holy Spirit are our hearts' true compass.

MARGARET SILF

Thy will be done

When we heard this, we and the people there urged him not to go up to Jerusalem. Then Paul answered, 'What are you doing, weeping and breaking my heart? For I am ready not only to be bound but even to die in Jerusalem for the name of the Lord Jesus.' Since he would not be persuaded, we remained silent except to say, 'The Lord's will be done.'

Today for the third time we hear the warning voices. All the people in the crowd add their voices to the weight of the argument against Paul's intended journey to Jerusalem. Paul has had enough of it. He responds to the storm of protest with a powerful statement of personal commitment, declaring that nothing is going to deter him and that he is ready to suffer any hardships that may befall him, even death itself, to do what he knows has to be done for the sake of the kingdom. Again we hear the echoes of Jesus' words, as he rebukes Peter so harshly for his attempts to dissuade him from going to Jerusalem (Matthew 16:23).

In the light of this courageous determination, the crowds are finally silenced. The only possible response is the response Jesus himself makes in Gethsemane, as he faces the full horror of his coming execution: 'Thy will be done.'

How often have we repeated this phrase in the Lord's Prayer? But have we ever reflected on what these words might actually one day demand of us? Jesus makes this act of surrender to God's will over and over again in the course of his earthly life, but surely the most agonising occasion would have been this fateful hour in Gethsemane when he still had the opportunity to choose otherwise. For Paul, too, there is still a chance to avoid all that lies ahead, but he will not be deflected from his chosen course.

Is there any situation in your life right now that needs you to trust the guiding of the Spirit and silence the human protest that might pull you off course?

Commitment is habit-forming. The more we are able to say
'Thy will be done' in small matters, the stronger we will be
if we are challenged by matters of life and death.

MARGARET SILF

Creative tensions

When we arrived in Jerusalem, the brothers welcomed us warmly… Then [the elders] said to [Paul], 'You see, brother, how many thousands of believers there are among the Jews, and they are all zealous for the law. They have been told about you that you teach all the Jews living among the Gentiles to forsake Moses, and that you tell them not to circumcise their children or observe their customs. What then is to be done?'

Most of us are inspired by stories of people who reach out to others in different cultures or traditions, making connections that bind humanity together as one family – those who challenge the conflicts between people of different world views and search for routes to reconciliation. They believe that what unites us as human beings is far greater than what divides us, and, like Paul, they act on that belief.

The brothers in Jerusalem are likewise inspired by Paul's ministry among the Gentiles, which strives to reconcile Jewish religious practice with the challenge to embrace Gentile converts, a mission that will inevitably attract opposition. Paul quickly comes up against the tension that occurs in such encounters. He is praised for all the conversions he has achieved among the Jews but also criticised for telling those living among the Gentiles to abandon some aspects of their faith practice. There is a tension between remaining fully observant of received tradition and enabling people of other persuasions to be welcomed, a struggle no less evident in our own times.

What, indeed, is to be done? Where is the space for fruitful compromise? What are the 'red lines' that must not be crossed? What can we learn from Paul in our own relationships with others who hold different worldviews?

Tension can be destructive, but it is also powerfully creative. Stringed instruments demonstrate this paradox very vividly. If the strings are too tight, they snap. If they are not tight enough, there will be no music. Paul is torn by tension that threatens to break him. He cannot know that future generations will rejoice at the music released into the world as a result of his struggle to reconcile these apparent opposites.

Working for reconciliation brings great heartache,
but yields a deeper harmony.

MARGARET SILF

Mob violence and fake news

The Jews from Asia, who had seen [Paul] in the temple, stirred up the whole crowd. They seized him, shouting, 'Fellow-Israelites, help! This is the man who is teaching everyone everywhere against our people, our law, and this place…' Then all the city was aroused, and the people rushed together. They seized Paul and dragged him out of the temple, and immediately the doors were shut.

Yesterday we reflected on how creative tension produces music, yet the sublime harmony of a concert performance is preceded by the discordant sounds of the players tuning their instruments. Such cacophony is nothing compared to the clamour that breaks out in today's reading. Everyone has an opinion about Paul and is determined to express it at full volume. Fake news abounds: reports of what Paul has actually said and done are shamelessly distorted and exaggerated.

As we read this, we are vividly transported back to the final week of Jesus' earthly life. First come the rumours and false accusations, scattered carelessly like kindling and set alight by sparks of jealousy and fear. The chance of a fair hearing is lost amid the lies being spread and amplified by an inflamed crowd, until, like Pilate, we are left asking 'What is truth?' (John 18:38). Law and order collapse into anarchy. Jesus' fate is handed over to the demands of a baying mob, and Paul is seized and dragged away behind closed doors.

It would not surprise us to see just such a scene enacted on the TV news. The doors that close on Paul are the doors of justice and of humanity. What happens behind those closed doors, we know only too well from our own troubled times. Paul is now walking his own *Via Dolorosa*. It is a path that each of us will walk at some time and in some form in our own lives. Perhaps you have your own experience of being falsely accused and being unable to defend yourself against lies and slander? Perhaps you know the pain of being harassed by people who make no effort to listen or understand? Perhaps you know the cruelty of those closed doors?

Let us beg for the grace to recognise and resist those
who stir up hatred in our own times.

MARGARET SILF

From conflict to conversation

Just as Paul was about to be brought into the barracks, he said to the tribune, 'May I say something to you?' The tribune replied, 'Do you know Greek? Then you are not the Egyptian who recently stirred up a revolt and led the four thousand assassins out into the wilderness?' Paul replied, 'I am a Jew, from Tarsus in Cilicia, a citizen of an important city; I beg you, let me speak to the people'… When there was a great hush, he addressed them in the Hebrew language.

Wednesday's reading ended with the rather desperate question: 'What then is to be done?' How do we begin to reconcile conflicting views? Today Paul shows us a way we can all explore. He asks for permission to speak. He initiates a conversation. As soon as there is a conversation, there is communication, inviting us to express our own thoughts and feelings and listen to the thoughts and feelings of others. Once this happens, things can change.

The tribune expresses surprise that Paul speaks Greek. This simple realisation immediately invalidates one piece of fake news: Paul can't be the Egyptian agitator they are looking for. With at least one aspect of the truth revealed, the conversation can continue. Paul identifies himself calmly, asks for permission to address the people and proceeds to spring his next surprise by speaking Hebrew. He is a Jew *and* a Roman citizen. These facts greatly strengthen both his credibility and his authority. Already the conversation is clearing away much of the debris of disinformation and distrust.

Genuine communication dissolves difference. As soon as a channel of authentic and honest communication opens, our crude assumptions break down. People we might have been inwardly tempted to dismiss, perhaps on account of something as superficial as their way of speaking, are discovered to be living beings with a story of their own that needs to be heard. When superficial differences fade into unimportance, bigger differences also soon cease to matter. We communicate more deeply, relating to each other as fellow human beings, beloved of God. Paul has surmounted an enormous hurdle, by speaking his truth and being heard.

May we help to turn conflict into communication and barriers into bridges in all our conversations.

MARGARET SILF

Paul's confession

When they heard him addressing them in Hebrew, they became even more quiet. Then he said: 'I am a Jew, born in Tarsus in Cilicia, but brought up in this city... educated strictly according to our ancestral law, being zealous for God, just as all of you are today. I persecuted this Way up to the point of death by binding both men and women and putting them in prison, as the high priest and the whole council of elders can testify about me.'

To the observant Jews he is addressing, Paul is presenting his credentials as one of them, brought up in strict obedience to the ancestral law. Indeed, his passion for the law had made him an active persecutor the people of the Way, many of whom he personally caused to be imprisoned and killed. To some of those present this would have been music to their ears. To us, as for Paul, it is a confession of the most extreme offences against humanity and, we would say, against God.

Here he is charged with compromising Jewish practice and giving Gentile converts what his detractors regard as a diluted version of Judaism. Their view would be that if Gentiles truly want to follow Judaism, they must comply with all its strictures.

This is just as familiar in our world today, especially regarding refugees and migrants: 'If they want to live in our country,' some people say, 'they must adopt our customs and values.' Other voices are more moderate, encouraging people to integrate into the life of the new country, but also regarding it as unreasonable to insist that they merge seamlessly into existing systems. Paul is trying to encourage his fellow Jews to adopt this more flexible approach as they welcome Gentiles into their faith communities. Tomorrow we will learn what brought him to this radical change of heart.

Meanwhile we might reflect on this question: when strangers seek to be accepted into our community, church or society, do we set them an entrance test first, or do we open our arms in welcome before we offer them whatever insight they might seek into our way of doing things?

May we be mindful of Paul's experience as we welcome strangers into our own communities.

MARGARET SILF

The road to Damascus

'While I was on my way and approaching Damascus, about noon a great light from heaven suddenly shone about me. I fell to the ground and heard a voice saying to me: "Saul, Saul, why are you persecuting me?" I answered, "Who are you, Lord?" Then he said to me, "I am Jesus of Nazareth whom you are persecuting"… I asked, "What am I to do, Lord?" The Lord said to me, "Get up and go to Damascus; there you will be told everything that has been assigned to you to do." Since I could not see because of the brightness of that light, those who were with me took my hand and led me to Damascus.'

The phrase 'the road to Damascus' has passed into everyday English usage to describe any startling, enlightening and life-changing moment. People who have never heard of the apostle Paul could tell you about 'road to Damascus' moments in their own lives.

Unfortunately many people assume that 'conversion' is only authentic if it comes at a particular moment and with earth-shaking force. Yet these events that change our lives come in an infinite variety of forms – perhaps moments in the natural world that spark new light within us, or times of deep grief or overflowing joy or gratitude. And sometimes they are simply moments out of time that envelop us, unexpected and uninvited, perhaps jolting us in a new direction or challenging us with new insight, leaving us in no doubt that we have felt the touch of God on our lives. And sometimes the touch of God is so powerful as to leave us feeling helpless in its radiance. Our own little light seems like a fragile candle, eclipsed by the rising of the sun.

What does 'Damascus' mean to you? How has God touched your heart in a personal, undeniable way? No one can ever take these moments from you. They are a unique, direct connection between you and God, as surely as Paul's encounter was for him. They change you forever in ways that may take a lifetime to discover. They light up your life for what seems like a fleeting moment but is actually a glimpse of eternity.

When has the light of God surprised you
and changed your own onward journey?

MARGARET SILF

Sight restored

'A certain Ananias, who was a devout man according to the law and well spoken of by all the Jews living there, came to me; and standing beside me, he said, "Brother Saul, regain your sight!" In that very hour I regained my sight and saw him. Then he said, "The God of our ancestors has chosen you to know his will, to see the Righteous One and to hear his own voice; for you will be his witness to all the world of what you have seen and heard."'

The explosion of light that robbed Paul of his sight on the road to Damascus has also opened his ears to hear the challenge of Jesus. It has, however, left him in a deep darkness. He needs to be led by the hand to Damascus. He is helpless to proceed in his own strength. The powerful persecutor of Christians has been put out of action in a flash of light, a single moment.

I understand that those who rescue people in danger of drowning sometimes have to immobilise victims before they can pull them to the shore. As long as we are proceeding under our own imagined strength we will continue to flounder in our own inner blindness and even struggle against those who would redirect our course.

Some of life's greatest blessings, however, begin and grow in the dark. Think of seeds, dreams and babies. Darkness forces us to let go of our control and makes free space for God to act. For Paul, the sudden plunge into darkness prepares the way for a new kind of light. Before his conversion, he possessed sight. After conversion, he is ready to move from sight to insight and Ananias is the chosen messenger of this change. The new insight is astounding. This arch-persecutor is being asked to become a witness of Christ to all the world.

Experience teaches us that we cherish the light that shows us the way, but find it harder to cherish the dark, even though it reveals the stars. Paul has temporarily lost the way, but he has glimpsed the stars.

God is able to call forth the best we can possibly be
out of the worst we are capable of becoming.

MARGARET SILF

The power of citizenship

The centurion… went to the tribune and said to him, 'What are you about to do? This man is a Roman citizen.' The tribune came and asked Paul, 'Tell me, are you a Roman citizen?' And he said, 'Yes.' The tribune answered, 'It cost me a large sum of money to get my citizenship.' Paul said, 'But I was born a citizen.' Immediately those who were about to examine him drew back from him; and the tribune also was afraid, for he realised that Paul was a Roman citizen and that he had bound him.

The question of citizenship is a big deal in our world today. Those who live in prosperous democracies often hear complaints about 'undocumented non-citizens' arriving on our shores and straining our resources. We assume that gives us the right to detain them or return them into dangerous situations.

We also know that for countless desperate people fleeing persecution or simply trying to survive in a ruthless world, the cost of 'documentation' can be exorbitantly high, as it was for the tribune in today's reading, who is about to unleash on Paul all the sanctions the Roman law permits, until Paul challenges him with the claim of citizenship. We who possess citizenship by birth may need to reflect on how we treat those who have to risk their lives to live in safety and freedom.

While challenging us to think prayerfully about our attitude to migrants and refugees, this incident also holds an amazing promise, far exceeding the issue of a visa: we are all citizens of the heavenly kingdom, and for this there is no 'large sum of money' to be paid. We are the children of God by birth, and this citizenship applies to every human being on planet Earth. No one is excluded at the border, because there is no border. Citizenship provides protection and the certainty of belonging, but it also requires us to offer the same protection and welcome to each other, without exception.

Roman law forbade the binding and flogging of a Roman citizen. The law of God just as surely forbids the maltreatment of any citizen of the heavenly kingdom – any child of God. What a difference it would make to our world if we respected this law.

MARGARET SILF

Conflict management

Paul… called out in the council, 'Brothers… I am on trial concerning the hope of the resurrection of the dead.' When he said this, a dissension began between the Pharisees and the Sadducees, and the assembly was divided…. Then a great clamour arose, and certain scribes of the Pharisees' group stood up and contended, 'We find nothing wrong with this man. What if a spirit or an angel has spoken to him?'… The tribune, fearing that they would tear Paul to pieces, ordered the soldiers to go down, take him by force, and bring him into the barracks.

From the beginning, the Christian church, in common with all institutions, has been marked by conflict and dissension. In today's reading Paul raises the question of belief in resurrection, suggesting that this is the reason for the action against him. In claiming the truth of the resurrection, he knows he is gaining the support of the Pharisees in the question of how to integrate Gentile converts.

There are no easy answers. The Pharisees believed in both resurrection and angelic spirits. The Sadducees believed in neither. Small wonder that 'the assembly was divided'. Matters become so heated that Paul has to be taken into protective custody before the warring factions tear him apart.

The 'tearing apart' continues in our own times, as people are demonised because of the opinions they hold. Tragically it is not uncommon to hear of people being driven to self-harm and suicide because they have been 'torn apart' on social media or by the press. Indeed, whole countries can be torn apart by political or social polarisation.

How can we move beyond this kind of violence? Paul has to be protected from its worst excesses, and we too are challenged to consider how we can protect the most vulnerable. Perhaps one comment from the camp of the Pharisees might help: instead of coming to blows over differing viewpoints, might we learn to listen respectfully to the opinions of others, keeping in mind that, just possibly, the Holy Spirit is at work in their hearts too?

The answers to our deepest questions are never black and white, but usually come in all the colours of the rainbow that appears when the Holy Spirit shines through our differences.

MARGARET SILF

Speaking up for justice

The son of Paul's sister heard about the ambush; so he went… and told Paul. Paul called one of the centurions and said, 'Take this young man to the tribune, for he has something to report to him'… The tribune… drew him aside privately, and asked, 'What is it that you have to report to me?' He answered, 'The Jews have agreed to ask you to bring Paul down to the council tomorrow… But do not be persuaded by them, for more than forty of their men are lying in ambush for him.'

When conflict has become so entrenched and there is evidence of serious wrongdoing, more drastic action is needed. Paul finds himself in a dangerous situation and unable to do anything to help himself. Some kind of intervention is needed if he is to have any chance of justice and freedom.

The intervention comes by the grace of God and the action of Paul's nephew, who demonstrates laudable loyalty in approaching the authorities on his uncle's behalf, as well as remarkable courage, in what we would now call 'whistle-blowing'. He knows that the conspirators have vowed to go on hunger strike until they have killed Paul, and they intend to trick the tribune into bringing him before the council. He informs the tribune of the conspiracy and urges him not to be deceived.

The tribune gives him a fair hearing, but sounding such warnings doesn't always proceed so smoothly. People who have the courage to speak out in our own times about what is out of order are often demonised and actively obstructed. Their desire to speak the truth may cost them their livelihood, their reputation and even, in extreme cases, their life. This otherwise unknown young man comes out of the shadows to speak up for justice.

In all human communities there will always be a few who conspire to do wrong. There will always be a few who have the courage to expose and challenge that wrongdoing. And there will always be the large, but silent, majority who don't want to get involved.

How, I ask myself, would I act in such circumstances?

Speaking out against injustice would be a very lonely place,
if God were not in the heart of it.

MARGARET SILF

The case for the prosecution

'Your Excellency, because of you we have long enjoyed peace, and reforms have been made for this people because of your foresight. We welcome this in every way and everywhere with utmost gratitude. But, to detain you no further, I beg you to hear us briefly with your customary graciousness. We have, in fact, found this man a pestilent fellow, an agitator among all the Jews throughout the world, and a ringleader of the sect of the Nazarenes. He even tried to profane the temple, and so we seized him.'

As we approach the end of our journey through these chapters of Acts, we find two starkly contrasting statements.

The first is by Tertullus, a renowned lawyer brought in by the high priest Ananias to present the case against Paul to the Roman governor. Tertullus begins with a sickening show of obsequiousness towards Felix, describing him as a peacekeeper and visionary reformer, worthy of the gratitude of all his subjects. All of this is, in fact, a total fiction. The Roman occupation and governance were almost universally hated, and Felix was no exception. There was no excess of gratitude in a territory that was, as was well-known, under constant threat of insurrection by a disgruntled populace.

Perhaps realising that Felix is unimpressed by his flattery, Tertullus turns to the matter of Paul. His accusations are as far wide of the mark as his earlier flattery had been. Inflated declarations usually have the ring of falsehood about them. In our world today we have been painfully reminded of the potentially destructive power of language. Words like 'rabble-rouser', 'ringleader' and 'pestilent fellow' are deliberately chosen to denigrate the person being accused, and set hearts and mind against him. Tertullus' lies about Paul cunningly focus on the very issue most likely to rouse the worst fear of the Roman governor – the fear of insurrection.

Extravagant or inflammatory rhetoric is never to be trusted. Those who are dishonest when bestowing praise will also be dishonest when apportioning blame. Their witness, whether positive or negative, is always a false witness.

Whether we express praise or criticism, may our hearts and our words always be guided by truth, sincerity and honesty.

MARGARET SILF

The case for the defence

Paul replied: 'I cheerfully make my defence, knowing that for many years you have been a judge over this nation. As you can find out, it is not more than twelve days since I went up to worship in Jerusalem. They did not find me disputing with anyone in the temple or stirring up a crowd either in the synagogues or throughout the city… I worship the God of our ancestors, believing everything laid down according to the law or written in the prophets… Therefore I do my best always to have a clear conscience towards God and all people.'

The motto of my old school was drawn from John 8:32: 'The truth shall set you free.' These words were engraved on our blazers and on our hearts and the years have never diminished their impact for me.

Yesterday we heard the angry, inflated speech of Tertullus. Today we move on to the 'cheerful', measured and understated response of Paul, who refuses to flatter the governor and proceeds to refute the accusations made against him. Paul quite simply calls upon the truth. He knows that the allegations against him are false, just as his accusers know it. He knows that, far from being a 'pestilent fellow', he has simply been carrying out the duties of an observant Jew in the local synagogues. As for the charge of being the ringleader of a potentially dangerous 'sect', he sets out his own beliefs clearly and honestly. There is no case to answer. He is answerable only to his conscience before God, for it is there that truth resides.

Five hundred years ago, Ignatius Loyola compared the effect of a destructive spirit to the sound of water splashing noisily on a stone, while the effect of the Holy Spirit resembles the action of water soaking gently into a sponge. Bluster and inflated rhetoric usually signify duplicity. Honesty and moderation are the mark of good faith and a clear conscience.

At the end of this brief journey, let us pause to reflect on what Paul's story has revealed to us, asking the Holy Spirit to bring fresh insight and renewed fervour to our faith and to guide us ever more deeply into the way of all truth.

MARGARET SILF

Unfamiliar voices of the New Testament

In the television quiz show *Pointless*, which I occasionally watch with my family, the aim of the game is to find the most obscure correct answer of a specific category. For example, one might be asked for the most obscure word ending in '-eek' or the most obscure type of DIY tool. The questions which always annoy me are the ones asking for characters in a well-known book, such as *Oliver Twist* or *Pride and Prejudice*. I have read and loved these books, but can never remember the names of the coffin-maker's maid (Charlotte) or Elizabeth Bennet's aunt (Mrs Gardiner). Yet the role they play is vital – adding colour and depth to the plot, enabling the author to highlight a character trait of the main protagonist, bringing humour, pathos and a whole host of other emotions into the reader's imagination as the story plays out across the pages of the book.

Over 3,000 different people are mentioned in the Bible. Some of these are known to almost everyone – Adam and Eve, Joseph, Moses, David, Jesus… But others would doubtless be 'pointless' answers. Barely described, meriting perhaps only a line or two in a chapter, nonetheless every one of these characters contributes to the overarching story of God's plan for the salvation of the human race. Some of these biblical heroes don't even have their names recorded, but we know that their names are written in the Book of Life, along with the names of others too numerous for human measures but each indescribably valuable to God.

As we explore what some of these minor players have contributed to our understanding and appreciation of God's saving work, we can allow the gifts and insights that they bring to shine a light on the 'minor characters' in our own life stories. These are the people who each day serve and support us, encourage and nurture us, sharing our lives in ways which should not be unnoticed but instead recognised and celebrated. And just as Christ himself noticed those on the outskirts of society, so we should take care to acknowledge those on the margins of our own lives, recognising the significance of each one in the eyes of God.

SALLY WELCH

Zebedee

As [Jesus] walked by the Sea of Galilee, he saw two brothers, Simon, who is called Peter, and Andrew his brother, casting a net into the lake – for they were fishermen. And he said to them, 'Follow me, and I will make you fish for people.' Immediately they left their nets and followed him. As he went from there, he saw two other brothers, James son of Zebedee and his brother John, in the boat with their father Zebedee, mending their nets, and he called them. Immediately they left the boat and their father, and followed him.

Poor old Zebedee – forever remembered as the one who didn't get out of the boat! The one who did not respond to the call of Christ. While four spring to their feet, one hesitates. Four drop their nets; one isn't quite ready to let go. And perhaps we can relate to that – perhaps all of us have been known to sit in the boat awhile and think about things. After all, to choose to follow Jesus is a major life decision. Discipleship requires dedication, work and sacrifice.

Christ calls countless times during our lives. Sometimes we are up to the task; other times we're not. Sometimes we are just not ready for adventure; other times we are following Jesus, but dragging our heels. Because we know that, while the call of Christ comes with the offer of abundant life, if we are to accept his offer, we must also accept some measure of risk. We are beckoned beyond the point of familiarity. We are asked to risk doing something we don't know how to do, to become someone we're not yet sure how to be. But it is at those moments that we would do well to consider safe old Zebedee, stuck in the boat, missing out on the biggest adventure of his life. He serves as a reminder that we cannot stay in the boat our whole lives and still find ourselves in the place where Jesus is going. We must follow.

And we would do well to consider above all that the risk we are taking on Christ is nothing compared to the risk he is taking on us.

Lord, help me to get out of my boat and follow you.

SALLY WELCH

Pilate's wife

So after they had gathered, Pilate said to them, 'Whom do you want me to release for you, Jesus Barabbas or Jesus who is called the Messiah?' For he realised that it was out of jealousy that they had handed him over. While he was sitting on the judgement seat, his wife sent word to him, 'Have nothing to do with that innocent man, for today I have suffered a great deal because of a dream about him.'

In Matthew's gospel, dreams play a significant role in the early years of Jesus' life. The magi are warned in a dream not to return to Herod after they have visited the new king, so they instead go home 'by another road' (Matthew 2:12). Thus Herod is prevented from discovering the actual location of this threat to his rule. Thwarted, Herod determines to kill one child by killing many, but once more a dream saves the infant Jesus as Joseph is warned that he must flee to Egypt (Matthew 2:13). Finally, it is through two further dreams that Joseph learns of Herod's death and returns to Israel to settle in Galilee. All who have experienced these dreams listen to their message and the benefits are made clear.

At the other end of his life, a dream has the potential to save Jesus once more. Pilate's wife warns Pilate because of her dream, but this time, the message is ignored, or at least not fully acted upon. Pilate does not rescue Jesus, but instead abnegates all responsibility for his fate, sending him on to his death, unwilling to risk the wrath of the crowd who have been stirred up against this strange prophet. Pilate's position is saved, but his name is held up forevermore as a particular type of cowardice, prepared to set truth aside in order to keep hold of power and position.

We may not hear warnings in dreams, but we will hear them in other ways: through the advice of friends or counsellors; through the words of the Bible or Christian commentators; through the inner promptings of our own conscience. We would do well to listen, to judge their righteousness and to act if necessary.

Lord, help me to hear your truth when it is spoken.

SALLY WELCH

The guards at the tomb

After the sabbath, as the first day of the week was dawning, Mary Magdalene and the other Mary went to see the tomb. And suddenly there was a great earthquake; for an angel of the Lord, descending from heaven, came and rolled back the stone and sat on it. His appearance was like lightning, and his clothing white as snow. For fear of him the guards shook and became like dead men.

My younger son is a sports enthusiast, both playing and watching, and in the evenings we often sit and catch up on the sporting events of the day. What a turmoil of emotion is exhibited during those broadcasts! The looks of joy on the faces of the winners, sometimes mixed with disbelief as if they cannot truly grasp that after the years of training, sacrifice and pain they have finally achieved their goals. Contrasting this are the looks of disappointment and misery on those who have failed to win a medal. Most poignant are those who have just missed out on success, whether through accident, injury or just failing to give enough finally to secure the triumph they have chased for so long. What courage and resilience it must take to pick oneself up after that, assess the failure and begin to train once more.

I am reminded of these sporting failures when I read this passage and reflect on the anonymous guards at the tomb of Christ. When he appears, risen from the dead, transforming everything that has been accepted about life, death and eternity, these hapless men faint from fear. Thus do they miss out on the greatest adventure of their lives. The women, on the other hand, stand firm and so are the first to hear those life-changing words: 'Do not be afraid; I know that you are looking for Jesus who was crucified. He is not here; for he has been raised, as he said' (Matthew 28:5–6).

The Christian journey is not always easy – the Way is strewn with difficulties and challenges, failures and defeats. But we must not lose heart or allow fear to turn us away from the true path. For those who keep going, the end will always be victory.

'I have finished the race, I have kept the faith' (2 Timothy 4:7).

SALLY WELCH

The lawyer

But wanting to justify himself, [the lawyer] asked Jesus, 'And who is my neighbour?' Jesus replied, 'A man was going down from Jerusalem to Jericho, and fell into the hands of robbers, who stripped him, beat him, and went away, leaving him half dead. Now by chance a priest was going down that road; and when he saw him, he passed by on the other side. So likewise a Levite, when he came to the place and saw him, passed by on the other side. But a Samaritan while travelling came near him; and when he saw him, he was moved with pity.'

I wonder what sort of reasons and arguments the lawyer presented before an imaginary court for the priest and the Levite as they ignored the suffering of the wounded man. Perhaps he sympathised with them – they were significant people; they must have had places to go and people to see. What a shock it must have been to him when he heard that the one who responded to the needs of another human being was the despised man, the outcast. How shaken must that lawyer have been as he tried to work out a new world view in the light of this story! We know he succeeds, as he acknowledges the truth which Jesus is teaching. Whether the lawyer did as Jesus commanded and actually went and did likewise, we don't know.

How do we behave when no one is watching? What acts of carelessness, idleness and selfishness do we commit when there is no possibility of comeback from them? What deeds of kindness, hospitality and generosity do we omit if there is no public obligation to perform them? C.S. Lewis wrote that 'integrity is doing the right thing, even when no one is watching'. When David the shepherd boy is anointed king, we are told that people 'look on the outward appearance, but the Lord looks on the heart' (1 Samuel 16:7). This is both a promise and a warning – we are accountable for our words and actions even when no one else can see, when we stop to help and when we walk on by.

'You are the God who sees me' (Genesis 16:13, NLT).

SALLY WELCH

The poor widow

[Jesus] sat down opposite the treasury, and watched the crowd putting money into the treasury. Many rich people put in large sums. A poor widow came and put in two small copper coins, which are worth a penny. Then he called his disciples and said to them, 'Truly I tell you, this poor widow has put in more than all those who are contributing to the treasury. For all of them have contributed out of their abundance; but she out of her poverty has put in everything she had, all she had to live on.'

Some years ago I was invited to lunch at the holiday home of a very wealthy family – actually, it was less a home than a castle, thoroughly modernised and truly splendid. After lunch I chatted to their six-year-old son. We talked about the usual things and then he asked me, 'Are you rich?' 'Yes I am', I replied. 'I have people to love, enough food and clothes, a job I like and a roof over my head. That's more than many people in the world.' He looked at me silently for a while, then spoke as he walked away: 'That's not rich. I am rich. Really rich.'

I was saddened by this conversation. At such a young age, this child was already seeing wealth solely in monetary terms and had already been taught to despise those who lacked such 'wealth'. And it is easy to criticise such people – perhaps less easy to see similar faults in our own behaviour. How often in our church communities do we sing the praises of wealthy donors who give large sums to specific projects, while ignoring the poorer members who faithfully give as much as they can? And in our personal lives, do we give more respect and pay more attention to those who are better off, more articulate or have greater status?

Jesus reminds us here that in God's kingdom, all are judged equally and the true cost of our actions are evaluated on heaven's terms, rather than those of this world. Let us pray that we are not found wanting in the final assessment.

Lord God, help me to give and not to count the cost.

SALLY WELCH

Jairus' daughter

Just then there came a man named Jairus, a leader of the synagogue. He fell at Jesus' feet and begged him to come to his house, for he had an only daughter, about twelve years old, who was dying… While he was still speaking, someone came from the leader's house to say, 'Your daughter is dead; do not trouble the teacher any longer.' When Jesus heard this, he replied, 'Do not fear. Only believe, and she will be saved.'

As you might know, this healing is sandwiched around the story of the outcast woman who suffered from a flow of blood. Touching Jesus' cloak, she is healed. Despite the crowd, Jesus notices the woman's actions and treats her gently – 'Daughter,' he says to her, 'your faith has made you well; go in peace' (Luke 8:48). Only then does Jesus continue on to Jairus' house, where it is not too late to save his daughter, and she too is healed.

The balance of these two stories is careful and gives us a powerful message. We recognise that even the richest, most influential of men is helpless when those he loves are threatened. We are all brought to the same level by the eternal truths of love, life and death. We learn that even the poorest and least powerful of women are valued by Christ, as he draws to him the outcast and the sick, the maimed and the damaged, and treats them just the same. Most importantly of all, perhaps, we learn that in the kingdom of heaven, it is not enough for just some to be whole, but that the welfare of each one of us depends on the well-being of all. Jairus' daughter is twelve years old – the same number of years that the woman has suffered. Before the daughter can be healed, the other daughter of Israel must also be cured.

In our fraught, pressured, individualistic society, it is easy to forget the good of the whole as we struggle each for their own. This story reminds us that a healthy community is one in which everyone can thrive, each person bringing what they can for the benefit of the group.

We share our mutual woes,
our mutual burdens bear,
and often for each other flows
the sympathising tear.
(John Fawcett, 1739–1817)

SALLY WELCH

Barnabas

As many as owned lands or houses sold them and brought the proceeds of what was sold. They laid it at the apostles' feet, and it was distributed to each as any had need. There was a Levite, a native of Cyprus, Joseph, to whom the apostles gave the name Barnabas (which means 'son of encouragement'). He sold a field that belonged to him, then brought the money, and laid it at the apostles' feet.

I read a piece of research recently on the effectiveness of leadership teams. Apparently the factor that made the greatest difference between successful teams and those that were less successful was the ratio of positive comments team members received about their work compared to negative ones. The highest performing teams received six compliments for every criticism. Conversely, those who performed least well got three negative comments for every positive one. The researchers concluded that some criticism was essential if a team was to perform well, but constant carping on minor matters destroyed team spirit and lowered efficiency. Far better was the judicious use of compliments to highlight and encourage good results rather than always pointing out mistakes.

We knew that already, didn't we? Anyone who has brought up children knows that encouraging good behaviour works better than punishing poor behaviour. But it also works within our communities – how much better it is to highlight the successes and achievements of a group of people than to draw attention to their deficiencies! We should be reflecting on our actions and always thinking of ways to improve them, but within the context of an affirming and supportive community rather than as part of an avoidance technique in an attempt to escape further criticism. This too easily leads to a 'siege mentality', where nothing new is tried and innovation is discouraged for fear of adverse and destructive comments.

Let us celebrate the Barnabas within us all – the encourager, the supporter, the uplifter. Let us be communities who do not condemn failure but use it as a springboard for success. Let us be like Christ, who gave Peter leadership of his sheep even after he failed him in his time of greatest need.

Lord God, help me to encourage, not to condemn.

SALLY WELCH

Ananias and Sapphira

After an interval of about three hours [Sapphira] came in, not knowing what had happened. Peter said to her, 'Tell me whether you and your husband sold the land for such and such a price.' And she said, 'Yes, that was the price.' Then Peter said to her, 'How is it that you have agreed together to put the Spirit of the Lord to the test? Look, the feet of those who have buried your husband are at the door, and they will carry you out.' Immediately she fell down at his feet and died. When the young men came in they found her dead, so they carried her out and buried her beside her husband.

This shocking tale is told immediately after we have celebrated the way in which the new followers of the Way share everything in common, and after we have heard about Barnabas the encourager. What a contrast is made – and what a warning to those who try to deceive God.

This tale is about more than simply the dishonest sale of some land, the murky attempt to defraud a community by keeping back money for personal use. It is a reminder that those who want to follow the way of the cross must be prepared to put everything they have into the journey. Nothing must be held back – all must be dedicated to the service of God.

This doesn't only apply to our gifts and talents, the good things that we bring. Our whole selves, even the unworthy parts, are to be refined and purified so that we can be truly redeemed and can inhabit our new lives with all our sins forgiven.

Not for nothing are we warned that those who wish to follow Christ must give their all: 'No one who puts a hand to the plough and looks back is fit for the kingdom of God' (Luke 9:62). These seem harsh words indeed, but we are reminded again and again of the greatness of the prize – for it is the kingdom of heaven which is at stake.

'The kingdom of heaven is like a merchant in search of fine pearls; on finding one pearl of great value, he went and sold all that he had and bought it' (Matthew 13:45–46).

SALLY WELCH

Gamaliel

But a Pharisee in the council named Gamaliel, a teacher of the law, respected by all the people, stood up and ordered the men to be put outside for a short time… 'So in the present case, I tell you, keep away from these men and let them alone; because if this plan or this undertaking is of human origin, it will fail; but if it is of God, you will not be able to overthrow them – in that case you may even be found fighting against God!'

The disciples are in Jerusalem, full of the Holy Spirit, healing the sick and spreading the gospel. They were imprisoned by the Jewish authorities, but overnight an angel opened the door and here they are again, preaching and teaching despite all threats and dangers, because, they say, 'We must obey God rather than any human authority' (Acts 5:29). Enraged, the Sadducees arrest them again and want them killed, but in steps Gamaliel, with these wonderful words of wisdom, freeing the disciples to continue their mission.

This short story, no more than an interlude in the thrilling adventure which is the book of Acts, has been part of the bedrock of my ministry. It has been so from the very beginning when, after months of hesitation, I finally approached my parish priest to tell him that I thought God was calling me to be a priest and, although I was really reluctant to explore this, I was willing to give the process a go until I was prevented from travelling further. Since then, many of my biggest steps in ministry have been taken with a similar approach, confident in God's purposes and trusting that if I had heard his message wrongly, I would be corrected, but that if I was carrying out his will, the project, the vision, the plan would proceed.

One of Christ's post-resurrection appearances is made to the disciples in Galilee. He commissions them to 'make disciples of all nations' and ends by reminding them, 'I am with you always, to the end of the age' (Matthew 28:19–20). What a promise!

Loving Father, help me to remember your presence and to have faith in your promises to me.

SALLY WELCH

Simon the sorcerer

Then Peter and John laid their hands on them, and they received the Holy Spirit. Now when Simon saw that the Spirit was given through the laying on of the apostles' hands, he offered them money, saying, 'Give me also this power so that anyone on whom I lay my hands may receive the Holy Spirit.' But Peter said to him, 'May your silver perish with you, because you thought you could obtain God's gift with money! You have no part or share in this, for your heart is not right before God… For I see that you are in the gall of bitterness and the chains of wickedness.'

One of the remarkable features of the NHS has been their vaccination programme. Year after year, hundreds of thousands of children and adults are inoculated against measles, typhoid, influenza and, more recently, Covid-19. These vaccinations are delivered free to those who need them on an incredibly fair basis of need and age. The Covid-19 vaccinations, for example, were given first to those with underlying health conditions which made them particularly vulnerable to the infection, then in order of age. Nothing else. Everyone, royalty, politicians, prisoners – whatever their wealth or status – had to wait until their age group was reached.

Salvation is distributed even more generously – not even age is a barrier! To everyone who asks, it will be freely given, and that point is repeated time and again throughout the New Testament. What we cannot do, however, is buy it, steal it, bribe others for it or exploit it, and Simon the sorcerer discovers this the hard way. Previously he had 'amazed' the people with his magic, but on hearing the good news from Philip he believes and is even baptised. But Simon has much to learn about the ways of the kingdom, part of which is that money holds no power there. Simon has yet to learn that this is one of the joys of the kingdom of God – open to all, free to all, God's grace is poured out upon those who need it. All we have to do is place ourselves before God and ask, in humility, with faith and hope.

'Pray for me to the Lord, that nothing of what you have said may happen to me' (Acts 8:24).

SALLY WELCH

Dorcas

Now in Joppa there was a disciple whose name was Tabitha, which in Greek is Dorcas. She was devoted to good works and acts of charity. At that time she became ill and died. When they had washed her, they laid her in a room upstairs. Since Lydda was near Joppa, the disciples, who heard that Peter was there, sent two men to him with the request, 'Please come to us without delay.' So Peter got up and went with them; and when he arrived, they took him to the room upstairs. All the widows stood beside him, weeping and showing tunics and other clothing that Dorcas had made while she was with them.

I have taken many funerals in my time as parish priest. Some are exceedingly hard – the deaths of those who have died before their time are anguishing and tear at the heart strings. Others, however, have an element of joy about them – none more so than when the deceased is a Christian at the end of a long, fulfilled life. Then the funeral becomes a thanksgiving for a life well lived, as their legacy of love and service is celebrated and the mourning community commit themselves to living in a way which honours their memory.

On the occasion told in Acts 9, Dorcas does not remain dead; she is healed by Peter and can once more carry out her good works and acts of charity. But this story demonstrates that while wealth and power have their impact, and can be used for good or ill in a community, equally valuable are those small, almost unknown acts of generosity and service – a kind word, a meal offered, a tunic made. So those of us who will never make the news headlines or be given public recognition for deeds of goodness or valour can nonetheless make a significant impact on the world around us, changing it for good, one small gesture at a time.

Little drops of water
Little grains of sand,
Make the mighty ocean,
And the beauteous land.
(Julia Carney, 1823–1908)

SALLY WELCH

Simon the tanner

Cornelius replied, 'Four days ago at this very hour, at three o'clock, I was praying in my house when suddenly a man in dazzling clothes stood before me. He said, "Cornelius, your prayer has been heard and your alms have been remembered before God. Send therefore to Joppa and ask for Simon, who is called Peter; he is staying in the home of Simon, a tanner, by the sea." Therefore I sent for you immediately, and you have been kind enough to come. So now all of us are here in the presence of God to listen to all that the Lord has commanded you to say.'

The story of Cornelius is a significant one in the book of Acts – the centurion is the first person who is not of the Jewish faith to hear the good news and believe that Jesus Christ is the Son of God.

At this stage in the story my mind doesn't fail to become distracted. Far from rejoicing at the beginning of the task of making disciples of all nations, I simply feel sorry for Simon the tanner. Living quietly in his house by the sea at Joppa, Simon has already put himself out by hosting Peter. This presumably involves not only accommodating him, with all that entails in terms of preparing and serving food and other domestic duties, but also providing all those who visited Peter with refreshments, making space for meetings and conversations, prayer groups and discussion.

And now suddenly four Gentiles arrive, no doubt also seeking hospitality, and Simon must risk uncleanness by allowing them to enter his house to meet with the man who has overturned all normal expectations with his news of the One who has overturned all expectations.

Let us give thanks for all those missionaries of the gospel, who serve not by preaching and teaching but by offering their homes and their possessions, their time and their money to enable others to hear the good news which is offered to all people. Let us remember the hosts of house groups, the makers of gallons of soup, the cleaners of buildings, the deliverers of leaflets… remember and give thanks.

Who sweeps a room as for Thy laws,
Makes that and th' action fine.
(George Herbert, 1593–1633)

SALLY WELCH

Rhoda

When [Peter] knocked at the outer gate, a maid named Rhoda came to answer. On recognising Peter's voice, she was so overjoyed that, instead of opening the gate, she ran in and announced that Peter was standing at the gate. They said to her, 'You are out of your mind!' But she insisted that it was so. They said, 'It is his angel.' Meanwhile, Peter continued knocking; and when they opened the gate, they saw him and were amazed.

The Bible isn't particularly well known for its moments of comedy, but this surely has to be one of them. To be fair to the hapless Rhoda, when you know for sure that a man is chained up inside a Roman prison cell, it can be extremely disconcerting to hear him knocking at your gate. But apart from lightening the mood, the tale of Rhoda has been included for good reason. First, she sticks to her story – against all odds it is indeed Peter who is standing outside the house, waiting to be let in. She doesn't allow anyone else's version of the truth to deter her but maintains her position.

More seriously, however, in her joy and confusion, she has kept the gate closed on this miraculous escapee. I am reminded of the parable of the sower and the seed in Matthew 13. Some of the seeds fell on rocky soil. 'They sprang up quickly... but when the sun rose, they were scorched; and since they had no root, they withered away' (Matthew 13:5–6). Are we being warned in the story of Rhoda that rejoicing in our faith is one thing, but we then need to act upon it? Rhoda must let Peter in – we must let Christ fully into our hearts and lives.

How much are we in danger of leaving Jesus at the gate of our lives, forever knocking at the door? We are full of joy at the message he brings, but how willing are we to allow our priorities, values and lifestyle itself to be transformed by his living presence?

'Listen! I am standing at the door, knocking; if you hear my voice and open the door, I will come in to you and eat with you, and you with me'
(Revelation 3:20).

SALLY WELCH

Onesiphorus

May the Lord grant mercy to the household of Onesiphorus, because he often refreshed me and was not ashamed of my chain; when he arrived in Rome, he eagerly searched for me and found me – may the Lord grant that he will find mercy from the Lord on that day! And you know very well how much service he rendered in Ephesus.

Some years ago, I was privileged to assist on a pilgrimage across the diocese of Oxford, from Radcot Bridge in the west to Wraysbury in the east. The bishop of Oxford led a party of pilgrims over ten days as the landscape changed from fields and woods to a more urban route, as we walked and talked and prayed our way along the Thames Pilgrim Way. At the end of each day's walk, weary pilgrims were welcomed by the local church community. We gathered in prayer and then chatted about the day's experiences over the most amazing teas I have ever eaten. Every kind of savoury dish, delicious cakes and pots of tea and coffee were offered to us by the hospitable 'home team', and we were extremely grateful.

On chatting with some of the hosts, I would often hear, 'I would love to have joined you but couldn't because…', followed by a reason, often very moving, for their inability to become pilgrims themselves. In response, I reminded them that they were a vital part of the journey, and their refreshment and encouragement gave us what we needed to set off the next day.

So too does Paul recognise Onesiphorus and his household for their part in Paul's missionary work. Not much is known about this man, but he seems to have been energetic and passionate in his desire to help Paul spread the news of Jesus' saving work. Not deterred by effort, he helps not only Paul but also the Christians in Ephesus as they explore what it means to be a follower of Christ. We don't know what type of 'refreshment' he brought to Paul, but whether it was physical or spiritual, the result was the same – through his service to one person, Onesiphorus enabled service to many.

Lord, let me serve you by serving others.

SALLY WELCH

Psalms 85—98

 Although it is about 60 years ago, I can still remember the first psalm that I played on the organ for a service: it was Psalm 65, the last verse of which reads: 'The folds shall be full of sheep; the valleys also shall stand so thick with corn, that they shall laugh and sing' (Psalm 65:14, BCP).

Why do I remember? It was a Harvest Thanksgiving service and of course that was and still is one the psalms appointed for use that day. I remember too that the Psalter we used was *The Cathedral Psalter with Chants* which was first published in 1902. I wonder how many of those are gathering dust in vestry cupboards? Even a bit of mildew!

In the intervening years many other psalters and new ways of singing the psalms have come along. I recall this not just out of nostalgia, but to help make the point that 60 years ago the diet of Sunday worship in most Anglican churches was matins and evensong and so we sang at least two psalms every Sunday – often more – plus the canticles. Those in the free church tradition had their metrical psalms.

The psalms are not quite as prominent in the average church today. Matins and evensong are a bit of a rarity outside cathedrals and, while the ministry of the word in the Eucharist includes a psalm, having been an itinerant preacher for 21 years, I can say with authority that many churches give them a miss!

Yet the psalms are important and valuable. When we sing or recite them we are joining in the songs of Christians down the ages – they are part of the historic worship of the church. They are spiritually important; Dietrich Bonhoeffer described them as 'the prayer book of the Bible'. They are deeply human in that they reflect and encourage us to reflect upon all types of human emotion, from utmost joy to total despair. They are God-centred in that they trace God's hand in the salvation of the world. Finally and significantly, Jesus made them his own, and when we use them we are using words precious to him.

Over the next two weeks, therefore, we will touch upon a few verses from each of 14 psalms and take time to ponder them and learn from them.

GEOFFREY LOWSON

Meeting and kissing!

Surely his salvation is at hand for those who fear him, that his glory may dwell in our land. Steadfast love and faithfulness will meet; righteousness and peace will kiss each other. Faithfulness will spring up from the ground, and righteousness will look down from the sky. The Lord will give what is good, and our land will yield its increase. Righteousness will go before him, and will make a path for his steps.

You will want to put memories of the Covid pandemic behind you, but dare I ask you to think back to the worst months of it? For my part I recall lamenting the situation in which we found ourselves, harking back to happier days before it came upon us, and looking forward to it being over. I hope that as you read this, it is a relatively distant memory – though it may not be!

I mention my reaction because it is helpful in illustrating the structure and message of today's psalm. It was written at a time of difficulty; we do not know what this was, though the reference to 'our land will yield its increase' suggests that the people had been through a famine. This time of trouble is lamented in the first half of the psalm and, as with my reminiscing above, there is a harking back to happier times before the disaster. But then the mood changes and a single voice proclaims some good news – 'salvation is at hand'; the glory that had departed will return for those in awe of God.

Then the psalmist goes on to portray salvation as four qualities – steadfast love, faithfulness, righteousness and peace. But more than that, these qualities are active and interacting, two of them 'meeting' and the other two 'kissing'. What a lovely optimistic picture with these qualities of God interacting to restore wholeness to the world.

The point the psalmist is making is that salvation is a dynamic, ongoing process; salvation happens when these godly qualities are active and working together in the lives of individuals and the community.

Lord of our life and God of our salvation,
Star of our night and hope of ev'ry nation:
Hear and receive your church's supplication,
Lord God Almighty.
(Philip Pusey, 1799–1855)

GEOFFREY LOWSON

Servant and Lord

Incline your ear, O Lord, and answer me, for I am poor and needy. Preserve my life, for I am devoted to you; save your servant who trusts in you. You are my God; be gracious to me, O Lord, for to you do I cry all day long. Gladden the soul of your servant, for to you, O Lord, I lift up my soul. For you, O Lord, are good and forgiving, abounding in steadfast love to all who call on you.

This prayerful psalm is attributed to David. It is as if he had a very early word processor, because there is a lot of 'cutting and pasting' going on, with verses from other psalms and from Exodus included! Here is a rich psalm that has much to teach us about prayer.

The prayer in this context is an appeal from a servant to the Lord; you will see above that the word 'servant' is used twice and 'Lord' three times; in the full psalm 'Lord' is used seven times and 'servant' three times.

Our present-day attitude to servants is coloured by history; we perhaps find the notion a little uncomfortable. But we must take care not to project that on to the Hebrew culture of the day. Then, the servant and master (lord) were in a sort of mutually beneficial relationship; the servant lived and worked for and towards the overall good of the lord. But in return the servant had the assurance of support and protection from his or her lord. It was a more positive dynamic than we might imagine.

In this psalm, the writer takes that understanding and applies it to the relationship between the one praying (the servant) and God, the Lord – with a capital 'L'. The servant is 'devoted' to the Lord and knows the Lord will respond.

And therein lies the power of this psalm. The servant (the writer) has complete and total faith and confidence in the Lord. The servant knows not only that the Lord can answer his prayers, but that he will.

The modern Hebrew Bible translates 'O Lord' as 'my Lord'. Reflect on this; does it add to your understanding of the relationship – of our relationship with our Lord?

GEOFFREY LOWSON

A wonderful mix

The Lord loves the gates of Zion more than all the dwellings of Jacob; her foundations are laid upon holy hills and he has made her his home. I will count Egypt and Babylon among my friends; Philistine, Tyrian and Nubian shall be there; and Zion shall be called a mother in whom men of every race are born.

We have a carver chair at home, which I refer to as 'the magic chair'. In my days with the United Society for the Propagation of the Gospel, we often entertained overseas clergy who were studying in this country. I would say to them, 'If you sit in that chair, you will become a bishop.' Naturally, much laughter ensued, but what I knew, or could guess at, was that they had probably been sent by their diocese to prepare for that very eventuality.

They were based at USPG's College of the Ascension in Selly Oak. I had the privilege of doing some additional study there for six months in 1984 and then visited regularly as part of my work. The college was in a federation of colleges initially established to prepare missionaries for work overseas, but by my time it was a community of church workers and potential leaders from about 60 countries, all involved in a range of programmes to help previously missionary-dominated churches shape themselves anew. It was a wonderful place. Christians of all races, denominations, traditions and cultures living, learning, sharing ideas and worshipping together.

Imagine you are the writer of our psalm today. You are in the temple for some great festival and you look around at those gathered with you and see people from all over the world – from Egypt, Babylon, Philistia, Tyre and faraway Ethiopia. The psalmist has this vision of people returning to Zion (Jerusalem) and being united through their love of the city and of God.

At Selly Oak, it was that sense of togetherness and common purpose that was so special and remarkable; it was not just about people coming from all over the world to be taught, but there was that mutuality – people learning from one another.

Let us give thanks for the richness and variety of the worldwide church, and pray for its unity.

GEOFFREY LOWSON

Still talking, still listening

O Lord, why do you cast me off? Why do you hide your face from me? Wretched and close to death from my youth up, I suffer your terrors; I am desperate. Your wrath has swept over me; your dread assaults destroy me. They surround me like a flood all day long; from all sides they close in on me. You have caused friend and neighbour to shun me; my companions are in darkness.

Almost all scholarly notes on this psalm begin with words along the lines of 'This is the saddest psalm in the whole Psalter.' In terms of categorising it, it is known as an individual lament. I like John Rogerson's terminology – 'a psalm of personal distress'. It really is 18 verses of gloom and doom with no relief.

That in itself is interesting, because individual lament psalms usually follow a pattern – they start by addressing God; then follows a complaint; then a request for help; next an affirmation of trust in God; and finally some vow along the lines of 'If you help me, I promise to…' But any positive ending is completely missing here, and we end up 'in darkness'.

We have to be honest and acknowledge that there are occasions when life does feel like this. Furthermore, for some people, for whatever reason, it feels like this a good deal of the time. I am sure you have met people for whom life seems to be a catalogue of troubles. There are times when it seems that God is totally silent. Some people appear to cope against all the odds, but others feel like our writer here.

In truth, the psalmist was being realistic about some aspects of our faith – there are times when our relationship with God is stretched. But that brings us to the nub of the psalm; the relationship may have been stretched, but the writer carried on talking right to the end. Despite everything he was still talking to God. In the light of what we know as post-resurrection people, we know that God would be listening and is still.

The poet Sylvia Plath wrote, 'I talk to God but the sky is empty.'
Reflect upon this.

GEOFFREY LOWSON

A positive answer: no!

How long, O Lord? Will you hide yourself forever? How long will your wrath burn like fire? Remember how short my time is – for what vanity you have created all mortals! Who can live and never see death? Who can escape the power of Sheol? Lord, where is your steadfast love of old, which by your faithfulness you swore to David? Remember, O Lord, how your servant is taunted; how I bear in my bosom the insults of the peoples.

I promise not to mention the pandemic again after today, but I wonder if, during those long months you ever uttered the words, 'How long, O Lord?' I know I did. It seemed as if it would never end. In this passage we have an even more anguished cry of 'How long?'

This lengthy psalm – 52 verses in total – begins by recalling God's promise of steadfast love and faithfulness towards his people, a promise sealed in a covenant with David. But some disaster has befallen the people, and so the writer laments the fact that God seems to have deserted his people; he seems to have forgotten the promise that he made. In the passage above, we have a direct appeal and a cry to God to remember what has gone before.

This plea to God to remember what he promised is a key part of this psalm because in a sense it both encourages us and gives us permission to make that plea to God in our own generation. On those occasions when we might feel that we have been abandoned, we can call on God to recall his promise. Equally important is that we also remember – remember that throughout history God has indeed proved trustworthy and true.

One final reflection, in response to the question 'Will you hide yourself forever?' As Christians we have an answer, which is an emphatic *no*. For we know that God revealed himself in a unique and special way.

Unlike God, we humans do break promises both as individuals and as groups or institutions. I have broken them – and others have broken their promises to me. As individuals, how do we react, how do we cope and how do we try to make recompense?

GEOFFREY LOWSON

Just passing through

Lord, you have been our dwelling-place in all generations. Before the mountains were brought forth, or ever you had formed the earth and the world, from everlasting to everlasting you are God... For a thousand years in your sight are like yesterday when it is past, or like a watch in the night. You sweep them away; they are like a dream, like grass that is renewed in the morning; in the morning it flourishes and is renewed; in the evening it fades and withers.

I have a particular affection for the Venerable Bede, the great seventh-century northern saint. As a student at Durham University, I attended what was then called Bede College. I taught for eleven years at Bede School in Sunderland. And for over 20 years my home was within a few miles of the monastery where he lived and worked.

Such is my affection that when I retired, as part of my very final evensong sermon, I read from Bede's *Ecclesiastical History of the English People*. I read the story which is often referred to as 'Bede's sparrow', in which he likened our life to the image of a sparrow flying in through the door of a banqueting hall with a feast in progress – flying around for a while and then flying out of another door. The sparrow just passed through. That is life. And in terms of my evensong sermon, the point was that I merely passed through that parish. When I had gone, the feast would continue.

The opening of our psalm today compares the eternity of God with the brevity of human life and indeed our mortality.

But there is more depth to Bede's story. For the pagan (as Bede would say), the sparrow comes from nowhere and goes out to nowhere and there is no knowledge of creation or the afterlife. Bede was able to persuade King Edwin that Christianity, wonderfully, gives some clarity to the before and after.

'I pray you, noble Jesus, that as you have graciously granted me joyfully to imbibe the words of your knowledge, so you will also of your bounty grant me to come at length to yourself, the fount of all wisdom and to dwell in your presence forever' (Bede, 673–735).

GEOFFREY LOWSON

Trust and confidence

Whoever dwells in the shelter of the Most High will rest in the shadow of the Almighty. I will say of the Lord, 'He is my refuge and my fortress, my God, in whom I trust.' Surely he will save you from the fowler's snare and from the deadly pestilence. He will cover you with his feathers, and under his wings you will find refuge; his faithfulness will be your shield and rampart.

My parents were farmers, but when I was very young they had to give up the farm and my father went to work in a green fruit warehouse. He did, however, keep a couple of fields with a few sheep and pigs, and we had hens at the bottom of the garden. Each spring Dad would watch out for a 'clucker' (a broody hen) and then get a clutch of eggs for her to hatch.

Then came the wonder and excitement of the chicks hatching out. I can still visualise them snuggled under the mother's wings for both warmth and security. It is a beautiful metaphor, and we are drawn to this cuddly image of warm protectiveness.

But we need to note that there are some stronger words used here too – fortress, shield and rampart all have military connotations. In describing the protection God offers, the psalmist is not talking of something wishy-washy, but rather something strong and powerful. Through his faithfulness God can give protection which is simultaneously gentle and strong.

There is another way to look at this: the chicks must have complete faith and trust in the mother hen and of course they do. However, Jesus uses this image in a strange way. In referring to those in the Jewish establishment in Jerusalem who had rejected him, he says, 'How often I have longed to gather your children together, as a hen gathers her chicks under her wings, and you were not willing' (Matthew 23:37). For God protects those who come to him in trust and confidence – just like the chicks.

Dear Jesus, as the hen covers her chicks with her wings to keep them safe, do thou this night protect us under your golden wings. Amen
(An evening prayer from India)

GEOFFREY LOWSON

A beautiful concept

It is good to give thanks to the Lord, to sing praises to your name, O Most High; to declare your steadfast love in the morning, and your faithfulness by night, to the music of the lute and the harp, to the melody of the lyre. For you, O Lord, have made me glad by your work; at the works of your hands I sing for joy.

I want to begin by recounting a story that I am sure many of you will recognise or may even identify with. An elderly neighbour died recently at the age of 86. She and her husband very cheerfully propped each other up for many years, but then she became totally dependent upon him and the carers – though inevitably the carers came and went. It was wonderful to witness the very practical care he offered – making her comfortable; preparing and serving up meals; seeing to those ordinary needs that he could manage on his own. He would even change for dinner each evening. It was a very practical sort of love – though there was always a Valentine card for her too!

From the biblical passage above, I want to focus particularly on the phrase 'steadfast love'. This term crops up 170 times in the Old Testament, 120 of which are in the book of Psalms. In the group of psalms covered over this fortnight, the phrase appears 16 times. It must have been important within the thinking of the Old Testament writers. (Some translations use 'loyal love', which I like.)

The Hebrew word which the NRSV translates as 'steadfast love' is *hesed*. It is an active word – not so much about feeling as doing. It denotes not merely an emotion, but action on behalf of someone who is in need. *Hesed* describes the love and loyalty that God gives us and which in turn inspires merciful and compassionate behaviour towards another person.

When I read the words 'steadfast love', I will think of my neighbour.

Reflect upon situations when you have witnessed steadfast love in others.

GEOFFREY LOWSON

King of all creation

The Lord has become King, clothed with majesty; the Lord is robed, girded with might. The earth is established immovably; your throne is established from on old; from all eternity you are God. Lord, the great deep lifts up, the deep lifts up its voice; the deep lifts up its crashing waves. Mightier than the sound of great waters, mightier than the breakers of the sea, mighty on high is the Lord. Your decrees stand firm, and holiness befits your house, Lord, throughout the ages.

It is thought that this psalm, which is categorised as an *enthronement psalm*, was part of an enthronement ceremony in the temple. But importantly and interestingly, it was God who was being proclaimed king. Just imagine some wonderfully rich service culminating in the words above – words which have power and splendour and which proclaim God as king of all creation.

This liturgy of 'enthroning God' probably began sometime after the return from the exile in Babylon. In fact, the Babylonians had a similar ritual, which the Israelites may have copied. But why would they want to do this? Throughout their history the Israelites had phases when they felt that God had lost interest in them and ceased to watch over them. They would speak of God being asleep or, as Bishop George Appleton put it, 'God had abdicated.' The period of exile in Babylon was one such phase, but the return marked the beginning of a new era, and God was seen as being in control, not just of Israel, but of the whole of creation.

The memorable story of Jesus calming the storm on the lake links back to the sentiments in this psalm. Jesus was asleep in the boat, but then woke up and took control, including commanding the elements. As our passage above reads, 'Mightier than the breakers of the sea... is the Lord.'

Finally, it is worth noting the groups of three in the passage – 'clothed', 'robed', 'girded'; three repetitions of 'deep'; three repetitions of 'mightier'. The writer really wanted to drive home a point.

Blessed are you, Lord God, King of the universe
Living and eternal God, rule over us always.
(Common Worship)

GEOFFREY LOWSON

Vengeance is mine?

O Lord, you God of vengeance, you God of vengeance, shine forth! Rise up, O judge of the earth; give to the proud what they deserve! O Lord, how long shall the wicked, how long shall the wicked exult? They pour out their arrogant words; all the evildoers boast. They crush your people, O Lord, and afflict your heritage. They kill the widow and the stranger, they murder the orphan.

In Roald Dahl's prize-winning children's book *Matilda*, the title character suffers from being mistreated, ignored and bullied by both her parents and her hideous headteacher Miss Trunchbull. Consequently, she takes her revenge in a variety of amusing ways, such as replacing her father's hair tonic with platinum hair dye. All great fun.

Yet vengeance is not an attractive thing, and the passage above talks of a God of vengeance. This can leave a justifiably unpleasant taste if read at face value, so it is important to understand that, as used in the Old Testament, 'vengeance' is not to be understood as 'getting your own back', nor a hateful reaction fuelled by emotion. Rather, it is a way of describing God's intention of re-establishing justice in situations where wickedness prevails. It is about God being in charge!

In yesterday's psalm we read of God being in charge of creation, which was expressed in terms of his being mightier than the seas. Today's psalm goes on to tell of God using his power to overcome the wickedness of the world: 'For the Lord will not forsake his people; he will not abandon his heritage; for justice will return to the righteous' (vv. 14–15). God is both creator and deliverer.

And what of *Matilda*? That, too, is a story of justice overcoming injustice. Miss Trunchbull is dismissed, and Matilda's parents end up in prison. Importantly, however, as the story progresses, Matilda moves away from that 'getting your own back' mentality. In Romans 12:19 we read, 'Do not take revenge, my dear friends, but leave room for God's wrath' (NIV).

Reflect on these words from Karl Barth (1886–1968):
'Shall I take the matter into my own hands? Shall I undertake to battle for right? Shall I become myself the invisible God?'

GEOFFREY LOWSON

In praise of singing

O come, let us sing unto the Lord, let us heartily rejoice in the strength of our salvation. Let us come before his presence with thanksgiving and shew ourselves glad in him with psalms. For the Lord is a great God and a great King above all gods. In his hand are all the corners of the earth and the strength of the hills is his also. The sea is his, and he made it and his hands prepared the dry land.

Childhood and teenage memories flood back whenever I hear these words, for we sang them every Sunday morning. Before the 1970s, the rural Church of England had not yet embraced the Parish Communion Movement, the aim of which was to make Holy Communion the main act of worship in a parish. Consequently, I was brought up on The Book of Common Prayer Morning Prayer, and the Venite (Psalm 95) featured in the service every week.

We had a choir of about ten, one of whom was Marjorie. She had a fine alto voice but sang loudly; she didn't always get the highest notes and set her own tempo. If the organist went fast, she went slower and vice versa. It is etched on my memory because I sometimes played the organ.

One suggestion is that this psalm was sung at the post-harvest Feast of Tabernacles, when the people recalled their time in the wilderness. And so, imagine if you will, the congregation gathering to enter the temple and then launching into this hymn of praise as they prepared to 'come before his presence with thanksgiving', or, as some translations have it, 'before his face'. What a wonderfully exciting image.

Marjorie departed this life over 30 years ago, and the village church in question rarely musters a *congregation* of ten, let alone a choir. But in mentioning her, I am emphatically not making fun of her or her singing. Quite the contrary, for she was a devout worshipper and really did 'sing to the Lord' and 'heartily rejoice'. This psalm has been used by the Christian church as an opening to worship from the earliest times, and Marjorie and countless others like her have been part of that.

'The singer himself is the praise contained in the song'
(Augustine of Hippo, 354–430).

GEOFFREY LOWSON

God is on a mission!

O sing to the Lord a new song; sing to the Lord, all the earth. Sing to the Lord, bless his name; tell of his salvation from day to day. Declare his glory among the nations, his marvellous works among all the peoples. For great is the Lord, and greatly to be praised; he is to be revered above all gods. For all the gods of the peoples are idols, but the Lord made the heavens.

If you would like to impress your friends at your Bible study group one evening, try (as if it were the most natural thing in the world) to slip the word *Heilsgeschichte* into the discussion! Joking aside, this word and the thinking behind it are worth a mention, particularly with reference to the little passage above, which talks about both 'salvation' and 'marvellous works'.

The German word translates as the interpretation of history emphasising God's saving acts and viewing Jesus Christ as central in redemption. It describes the notion that God does not act randomly in history; all his 'marvellous works' are not haphazard but are part of a great design. Some are encountered by his people in the ordinary events of life and may seem insignificant; others are more dramatic. But it is all part of God's saving plan, stretching from the time of Abraham until the fulfilment of the kingdom.

Today's psalm is another enthronement psalm, one of several in this selection, in fact (we considered the background on Monday). The writer reminds us that we must acknowledge God's saving activity, first by telling others about it, but also through praise and thanksgiving.

The psalm begins with this wonderfully excited threefold instruction to 'Sing to the Lord'. Further it is to be a 'new song', the significance being, again as we saw on Monday, the enthronement ceremony marked the beginning of a new era after the exile. A new start for the people of God.

God is working this purpose out, as year succeeds to year;
God is working this purpose out, and the time is drawing near;
nearer and nearer draws the time, the time that shall surely be:
when the earth shall be filled with the glory of God as the waters
cover the sea.
(Arthur Campbell Ainger, 1841–1919)

GEOFFREY LOWSON

A balancing act

The Lord is king! Let the earth rejoice; let the many coastlands be glad! Clouds and thick darkness are all around him; righteousness and justice are the foundation of his throne. Fire goes before him, and consumes his adversaries on every side. His lightnings light up the world; the earth sees and trembles. The mountains melt like wax before the Lord, before the Lord of all the earth.

'Away in a manger, no crib for a bed. The little Lord Jesus…' In all the main-stream churches, Psalms 96, 97 and 98 are those appointed for Christmas Day. Our psalm today, with all its powerful imagery, is read alongside Luke's story of the baby Jesus in the manger and the shepherds coming to visit. Images of infants with tea towels on their heads' springs to mind, and lovely it is too.

But one of the realities we have to acknowledge is that for many people – probably the majority – the only picture they have of our Lord is 'gentle Jesus, meek and mild'. They never get as far as the Jesus of Luke 4, where he proclaims that he has come 'to bring good news to the poor' (Luke 4:18) and much more.

In the passage above, God's majesty is portrayed through these wonder-ful figures of speech associated with a thunderstorm – clouds, darkness, fire and lightning – but nestled amid all of that is the statement that the foundation of the kingdom is righteousness and justice.

At Christmas, the wider world, and indeed the church itself, almost inevitably tends to focus on the baby in a manger. But in truth there is this juxtaposition of the vulnerable baby set alongside the one who is king and 'Lord of all the earth'. Jesus' *weakness* is evident at Calvary as well as the stable and so the infant son of Mary, the crucified Galilean and the 'Lord of all the earth' were all present at the beginning (John 1:1) and will be there at the end.

Reflect upon how you manage to hold these contrasting images together.

GEOFFREY LOWSON

Different sounds; the same purpose

O sing unto the Lord a new song, for he hath done marvellous things… Shew yourselves joyful unto the Lord, all ye lands sing, rejoice, and give thanks. Praise the Lord upon the harp, sing to the harp with a psalm of thanksgiving. With trumpets also and shawms, O shew yourselves joyful before the Lord the King.

I have always enjoyed the BBC's *Songs of Praise*. Indeed for many years a college friend was its producer. But over its 60 years it has inevitably, and rightly, changed – today there are far more praise bands and gospel choirs than traditional hymns. There are different sounds.

My wife is director of music at Barnard Castle Parish Church. The organ console (keyboard) is at the west end of the church and towering above her is the fine west window, part of which displays Moses' sister Miriam and other women playing instruments. Beside them there is a scrolled banner with the words 'Sing unto the Lord, for he hath triumphed gloriously'. Those words are from Exodus 15, but the sentiments are close to our psalm today.

Here we have yet another enthronement psalm and so imagine again some wonderfully rich service in the temple. But what did it sound like? The instruments were not as refined as today's, but a harp would sound like a harp, a timbrel like a cymbal. I wonder if the trumpets and shawms were quite in tune? But it does not matter: what matters is that we are called upon to respond to the marvellous things God has done and does by offering our praise and thanksgiving; we are encouraged to respond by being joyful and making music with both voice and instrument alike. It is both an obligation and a joy.

In our churches we do this season by season and the hymns, psalms and songs we sing now are an acknowledgement that, just as God was enthroned in the temple, he is also enthroned in our presence now.

Let all the world in ev'ry corner sing, 'My God and King!'
The church with psalms must shout: no door can keep them out.
But, more than all, the heart must bear the longest part.
Let all the world in ev'ry corner sing, 'My God and King!'
(George Herbert, 1593–1633)

GEOFFREY LOWSON

Hosea: wayward people, loving God

 I won't sugar-coat it – the book of Hosea has some tough passages to ponder. God speaks words of sadness through this prophet because of the ways his people fail him. As they give themselves over to other gods, worshipping idols through expressions of debauchery and sin, God feels the loss of their love. His anger burns against them, and he speaks words of judgement. But he never reaches the point of wiping them out forever. His love is too strong for that drastic action.

We're spending the first two weeks of Advent in this book of Hosea, and although we're not referencing this season in the notes, it is a good time to look at some hard truths. Doing so is countercultural, as people in December (myself included) often jump to the celebration of Christmas – with parties, meals and other events – and gloss over the true meaning of Advent. After all, Advent is about repenting and fasting, about waiting for the second coming of Jesus. Considering the anguish of God over his wayward people during this season can help us to examine the ways we fail him. As we turn from our sins, we can embrace the joy and feasting of Christmas all the more.

With the book of Hosea having 14 chapters, we move through it daily with excerpts from each consecutive chapter. Doing so helps us in the exercise of embracing the hard bits as well as God's loving words of forgiveness and restoration. We can form a fuller picture of why God is so unhappy with his people: they reject him again and again, relying on themselves in pride and turning to other loves. Thus when we read God's words of comfort, we see how deeply he grieves and just what it costs him to extend forgiveness.

As you prepare yourself to welcome God incarnate, the baby who is God, I invite you to consider the story of Jesus coming to earth from farther back. Because God's people left him heartbroken, he would set in motion the deepest expression of his love – sending his Son to become human, to die and to rise again.

May you experience a deep understanding of God's rich love for us,
his beloved, this Advent season.

AMY BOUCHER PYE

A hard call

The word of the Lord that came to Hosea son of Beeri during the reigns of Uzziah, Jotham, Ahaz and Hezekiah, kings of Judah, and during the reign of Jeroboam son of Joash king of Israel: When the Lord began to speak through Hosea, the Lord said to him, 'Go, marry a promiscuous woman and have children with her, for like an adulterous wife this land is guilty of unfaithfulness to the Lord.' So he married Gomer daughter of Diblaim, and she conceived and bore him a son. Then the Lord said to Hosea, 'Call him Jezreel, because I will soon punish the house of Jehu for the massacre at Jezreel, and I will put an end to the kingdom of Israel.'

This is not a very cheery start to our journey with Hosea! Although this prophet's name means 'salvation', his role is a tough one, as God calls him to be a living metaphor through his marriage to an unfaithful woman. He lives at the time of the divided kingdom, after Israel and Judah had split, and he dwells in the northern kingdom of Israel.

Hosea obeys God's call, marrying Gomer, and she bears three children, all of whom God instructs to give names that express his disappointment with his unfaithful people. Hosea is to name the firstborn Jezreel, which means 'scattered', indicating how God's people would be dispersed. Also, there will be a massacre at the Valley of Jezreel. He is to name the other children Lo-Ruhamah, meaning 'not loved', and Lo-Ammi, meaning 'not my people'. The Lord wants his people to see things from his point of view – to feel some of his heartache when they stray from his love.

As you ponder the hard path of Hosea, recall times when you've sensed God calling you to embrace something that was difficult or unexpected. Consider how you responded, and how God met you through that experience. As you look back, ask God to help you with any challenges you face currently, that you will have the strength to believe his promises.

Loving God, so often we fall short of your standards,
but you extend your loving forgiveness to us. Help me to embrace
your love and share it with others.

AMY BOUCHER PYE

Speaking tenderly

Therefore I will block her path with thornbushes; I will wall her in so that she cannot find her way… She has not acknowledged that I was the one who… lavished on her the silver and gold – which they used for Baal. Therefore I will take away my corn when it ripens, and my new wine when it is ready… I will stop all her celebrations: her yearly festivals, her New Moons, her Sabbath days… Therefore I am now going to allure her; I will lead her into the wilderness and speak tenderly to her. There I will give her back her vineyards, and will make the Valley of Achor a door of hope.

God continues to be disappointed with how his people reject him. They hanker after other gods, not acknowledging that he's the one who has delivered and saved them. With vivid language he declares how he will turn their face back to him: with thornbushes he will get their attention. Though the thorns may draw blood, they won't impart lasting damage. Indeed, God reveals his love even in this picture of walling them in. The prickly bushes not only ensure they'll receive his love but keep out the most undesirable creatures, such as foxes or other marauding animals.

Note how God says he will take away their fertile land, that which produces an abundance of corn and wine. He concludes that the only way they'll notice him is to let their crops fail. In times of hardship, they will more likely return to the Lord.

The words of God's judgement are stern and difficult, but he follows them with loving words of redemption – of how he will lure his people back to himself. He doesn't give up on those who stray from him but has a store of tender words for all who have turned away. Beckoning them back gently, he stretches out his open arms and yearns that they – that we – would return to his loving fold.

God, you are gentle and loving, speaking tenderly when I shirk your love as you call me back home. Help me to leave my attachments to false gods and find my rest in you.

AMY BOUCHER PYE

Saving God

The Lord said to me, 'Go, show your love to your wife again, though she is loved by another man and is an adulteress. Love her as the Lord loves the Israelites, though they turn to other gods and love the sacred raisin cakes.' So I bought her for fifteen shekels of silver... Then I told her, 'You are to live with me for many days; you must not be a prostitute or be intimate with any man, and I will behave the same way towards you.' For the Israelites will live for many days without king or prince... Afterwards the Israelites will return and seek the Lord their God and David their king.

The meaning of Hosea's name, 'salvation', comes to the fore in this passage, as God calls him to redeem his unfaithful wife. Although he could rightfully claim her as his own without payment, he buys her back. He promises to be intimate only with her, and he requests this of her. Again this lived-out metaphor paints a broader picture of the love of God for his wayward people.

Although God knows they will turn from him again and again, he offers to pay the price to have them return to himself. He knows that eventually they will seek him, although he will have to wait a long time. He yearns that they wouldn't prostitute themselves with other gods.

The promise of Hosea was true for God's people in those times, and he fulfils his promise to us through the sacrifice of his own Son, Jesus. He gives us his Spirit to help us stay true to him. How rich we are with resources to help us grow in the fruit of love, peace, joy and gentleness, among others. We need only to relinquish our need to be in control as we ask for his help each day. Perhaps, however, bowing our knees and asking him to take over might feel very hard. If so, we can ask for help with that big step, too.

Saving Lord, you have paid the ultimate price so that I can be at peace with you. Help me to relinquish every right I have claim to, that I will live wholeheartedly for you.

AMY BOUCHER PYE

The land dries up

Hear the word of the Lord, you Israelites, because the Lord has a charge to bring against you who live in the land: 'There is no faithfulness, no love, no acknowledgment of God in the land. There is only cursing, lying and murder, stealing and adultery; they break all bounds, and bloodshed follows bloodshed. Because of this the land dries up, and all who live in it waste away; the beasts of the field, the birds in the sky and the fish in the sea are swept away.'

Before our current climate crisis, God saw the impact of humanity on the earth. As he says through Hosea, the land dries up because of the lack of faithfulness and love, and because his people turn from him. All living creatures feel the effects of sin. So too for us: the more we seek to acquire, the more our beloved globe suffers. When we turn from God and ignore his ways, we waste our natural resources and spew out pollution on his beautiful earth.

We can repent of these actions, and we can pray for the healing of the earth. A 20th-century Christian, Agnes Sanford, prayed along these lines, believing that God was calling her to pray daily for the gentle release of tension in the earth's crust. To do so she moved near to the San Andreas Fault in California. We don't know how God answered those prayers, but it is a fascinating idea to pray in this way, especially as we seem to be hit with so much extreme weather. Wildfires, floods, hurricanes, tornados and so many other natural disasters wreak havoc on people, land and sea.

How might God respond to your prayers for places and people you're concerned about? Although we can't answer that question definitively, we can dream about how we can partner with him to bring restoration and hope to the land and its inhabitants.

Creator God, you made the world and all that is within it. How you must grieve at the destruction we bring about. Help me to be aware of my actions and their impact; help me to work with you for the healing of the earth.

AMY BOUCHER PYE

Moths and rot

Ephraim is oppressed, trampled in judgement, intent on pursuing idols. I am like a moth to Ephraim, like rot to the people of Judah. When Ephraim saw his sickness, and Judah his sores, then Ephraim turned to Assyria, and sent to the great king for help. But he is not able to cure you, not able to heal your sores. For I will be like a lion… I will carry them off, with no one to rescue them. Then I will return to my lair until they have borne their guilt and seek my face – in their misery they will earnestly seek me.

Hosea's prophecy continues to be difficult, with God pouring out words of anguish and judgement over his people. And yet; and yet. As we read the final words of this chapter, we learn that although his people suffer sores and sickness, they will seek his face in their misery. God doesn't want them to endure this pain, but knows that through it they can return to him.

Ephraim is one of the tribes of Israel, so we see that both the northern and southern kingdoms have removed themselves from God and his influence. Instead they engage in corruption, war with other nations and seek the help of other kings. In short, they prostitute themselves to other gods.

The true God seems to have had enough, wanting to remove himself from them. The image of him being a moth can startle us – an insect that is seemingly innocuous yet which wreaks destruction, one nibble at a time. Moths destroy as do floods and tsunamis, although on a slower and smaller scale. But God longs for his people to reveal their guilt and to seek his face; to repent and return to him.

We might not scurry after other gods in the way that God's people at the time of Hosea did, but yet our hearts long for fulfilment – whether through relationships, our work, gratification of our bodies or other things. Augustine of Hippo's words still resonate: 'Our hearts are restless, until they can find rest in you.'

Forgiving God, keep me from the moths that destroy. Help me to return to you with all my heart, finding peace and belonging.

AMY BOUCHER PYE

Mists and rains

Come, let us return to the Lord. He has torn us to pieces but he will heal us… After two days he will revive us; on the third day he will restore us, that we may live in his presence. Let us acknowledge the Lord; let us press on to acknowledge him. As surely as the sun rises, he will appear; he will come to us like the winter rains, like the spring rains that water the earth. What can I do with you, Ephraim? What can I do with you, Judah? Your love is like the morning mist, like the early dew that disappears… I desire mercy, not sacrifice, and acknowledgement of God rather than burnt offerings.

The conversation between Hosea and God continues, with Hosea seeking repentance from God's people. With his line about restoration on the third day, he foreshadows the redemption to come through Jesus. And he looks to nature to call the people to return to God, knowing that even as the sun appears each day, so too will God meet his people. Hosea believes that even in times of drought, the rains will reappear to water the earth, bringing nourishment and relief.

But God despairs at his wayward children. He too employs pictures from nature, saying that their love is as fleeting as the morning mist, which the sun soon burns away. How fragile our affections must appear to the unchanging God!

God knows that we often try to earn his love. But as he says through Hosea in this passage, and as Jesus later quotes twice to the Pharisees (Matthew 9:13; 12:7), God desires not sacrifice but mercy; he seeks our acknowledgement of him rather than frenetic activity.

Just as Hosea desired that Gomer would commit herself to her husband with all her heart, soul and body, so too does God long for us to serve and honour him. When we do so, we'll find ourselves immersed in his soaking spring rains. His living water will cleanse us and slake our thirst.

Lord Jesus, you said that you desire mercy not sacrifice. Show me what this means in my life today, that I might follow you fully, in my thoughts, words and deeds.

AMY BOUCHER PYE

Turning from God

They are all adulterers, burning like an oven whose fire the baker need not stir from the kneading of the dough till it rises… Ephraim is a flat loaf not turned over… Israel's arrogance testifies against him, but despite all this he does not return to the Lord his God or search for him. Ephraim is like a dove, easily deceived and senseless… When they go, I will throw my net over them; I will pull them down like the birds in the sky… Woe to them, because they have strayed from me!… I long to redeem them but they speak about me falsely.

Many images fill this section of Hosea, such as those around baking. Because the tribes of Israel are not true to God, they burn with desire for other gods, hot like coals ready to receive bread for baking. The 'flat loaf' that Hosea refers to relates to a dough that is half-cooked. In those days, bakers would produce something similar to a pancake, cooked on each side. Because the tribe of Ephraim wouldn't submit to God, they wouldn't be baked through, like a pancake that's done on one side but which oozes on the other.

God moves to the image of doves. These birds flock together and fly around aimlessly, and God throws his net over them, capturing them and pulling them down out of the sky. He burns with anger at their wayward hearts.

Yet even with these disturbing images, we see a spark of hope – of how God longs to redeem his people. They speak lies about him, but he doesn't give up hope that they will return and recommit themselves to him.

Pride kept God's people from following him in Hosea's day, and pride keeps our necks stiff, with us unwilling to bow our heads in humility and service. We might feel we are self-sufficient, not needing God's help. Yet we do. Take a few moments to review with God your passions and actions, asking him through his Spirit to reveal any areas where you might need to return to him.

'As far as the east is from the west, so far has he removed our transgressions from us' (Psalm 103:12).

AMY BOUCHER PYE

Sowing and reaping

They sow the wind and reap the whirlwind. The stalk has no head; it will produce no flour. Were it to yield grain, foreigners would swallow it up. Israel is swallowed up; now she is among the nations like something no one wants. For they have gone up to Assyria like a wild donkey wandering alone. Ephraim has sold herself to lovers. Although they have sold themselves among the nations, I will now gather them together. They will begin to waste away under the oppression of the mighty king.

More than once, God employs the metaphor of sowing seeds in the Bible. Here in Hosea he uses the image as a warning: that those who sell themselves to other nations will sow the wind and reap the whirlwind, their livelihood ruined. What they harvest will be worth nothing. Even if it could be salvaged, those whom they invited into their fields would swallow up any remaining goodness.

Again we glimpse a sliver of hope in one short phrase – 'I will now gather them together.' Even though they've brought this whirlwind upon themselves, God will have mercy. Like a farmer scooping up the seeds that he intends to sow in good soil, so the Lord gathers his wayward children from the dire places they have scattered. He removes the choking weeds that stifle their faith. He sends us the sunshine and rain to help the seeds grow and fortifies their soil with good nutrients, sometimes made from the compost of their lives.

Pause to ponder seeds, sunshine and the master gardener. If with the help of the Holy Spirit you were to picture your heart as a garden, what would it look like? You might see wild areas of colourful flowers and towering trees providing plenty of shade or neat and tidy sections of plants, highly cultivated. If you spot any weeds threatening to choke the fruitful vines, ask God to help you eradicate them. Know that God can make your garden a safe place for you to flourish and to welcome in others.

Loving Lord, I know that pruning is painful at the moment, but that growth will follow in time. Help me to bear fruit that lasts.

AMY BOUCHER PYE

The prophet a fool

The days of punishment are coming, the days of reckoning are at hand. Let Israel know this. Because your sins are so many and your hostility so great, the prophet is considered a fool, the inspired person a maniac. The prophet, along with my God, is the watchman over Ephraim, yet snares await him on all his paths, and hostility in the house of his God. They have sunk deep into corruption, as in the days of Gibeah. God will remember their wickedness and punish them for their sins. When I found Israel, it was like finding grapes in the desert; when I saw your ancestors, it was like seeing the early fruit on the fig-tree.

You may be growing weary of God stating his case against his people. The tone will change, but again we have to consider the sins of Israel and Judah. Their unfaithfulness reaches a new peak when they turn God's feast days into a mixture of worshipping the true God alongside idols – they revere Baal, the one from whom they seek a fruitful harvest. What was once a festival of true worship descends into a time of drunkenness and sexual orgies. God isn't happy about it.

Their disobedience means that God's people even take the prophet for a madman. No longer do they listen to his words of warning nor repent in sorrow. Though Hosea is God's appointed person, they greet him with disbelief and anger. Hosea despairs, as does God. The prophet asks God to reject his people; to make them wanderers among the nations. But however much betrayed, the Lord never gives up. He remembers the good times, such as when he discovered them, he felt like he was finding grapes in the desert.

Though the sins of God's people are wearisome, so are our own sins. We can find hope in the fact that God never gives up on his people – and he'll never desert us either. We too can be as refreshing as plump and juicy grapes in an arid land.

Tender Lord, thank you for loving me so much that you run towards me when I so much as shift my gaze to you. I seek your loving arms and welcome.

AMY BOUCHER PYE

Sowing righteousness

Ephraim is a trained heifer that loves to thresh; so I will put a yoke on her fair neck. I will drive Ephraim, Judah must plough, and Jacob must break up the ground. Sow righteousness for yourselves, reap the fruit of unfailing love, and break up your unploughed ground; for it is time to seek the Lord, until he comes and showers his righteousness on you. But you have planted wickedness, you have reaped evil, you have eaten the fruit of deception.

Each January I like to choose a word for the year and an accompanying verse. One year my scripture text was Hosea 10:12, and I was pleased with the imagery of sowing seeds of righteousness. Later I preached on this passage, speaking of the work of ploughing and planting. But in focusing on this verse, I too easily skimmed over the hard bits of judgement in this chapter of Hosea.

Now I see how we need to consider the larger picture of God's sadness over the sins of his people. After all, Israel and Judah haven't turned from their errant ways but remain a spreading vine more like a weed than something that is fruitful. As his people plant wickedness, they reap evil, bearing no good fruit.

Although we can't ignore the difficult bits, we can take encouragement from God's words about reaping the fruit of unfailing love. With his help we break up the crusty ground of unforgiveness, selfishness, anger, bitterness and control; we can ask God to send showers of healing, love, grace and peace. Having done so, we trust that he will answer our prayers.

You could take this passage, perhaps starting with 'Sow righteousness…', and ask God to help you digest its truth. One way is to write it out as a prose poem; another is to doodle the various words on a page. Stopping to ponder the images can help us to pause and receive from God.

Lord, I want to sow seeds of righteousness. Help me to break up any sin in my life, that I will bear the fruit of the Spirit. I want to work for unity and peace among those I meet.

AMY BOUCHER PYE

Cords of kindness

When Israel was a child, I loved him, and out of Egypt I called my son. But the more they were called, the more they went away from me. They sacrificed to the Baals and they burned incense to images. It was I who taught Ephraim to walk, taking them by the arms; but they did not realise it was I who healed them. I led them with cords of human kindness, with ties of love... How can I give you up, Ephraim? How can I hand you over, Israel?... My heart is changed within me; all my compassion is aroused. I will not carry out my fierce anger... For I am God, and not a man – the Holy One among you.

God's outpouring of compassion reminds me of the cool weather ushered in after intense heat and a thunderstorm. The Lord's anger over the betrayal of his people dissipates and his love oozes forth as the picture Hosea employs changes from lovers to father and child. The perfect love of a father shows forth in the compelling images of the 'cords of human kindness', the 'ties of love'. Last week we saw how God boxed in his wayward people with the thornbushes; here the image changes to a gentler one. I think of a fenced-in garden to keep a toddler from wandering off or a swimming pool enclosed by a wall to keep a child out of harm's way.

Why the change? 'For I am God, and not a man.' Because God loves so deeply, he forgives the wrongdoing of his people completely and doesn't carry out the consequences of his fierce anger. Instead, his compassion is aroused; he is a loving parent who wants the best for his children.

Sometimes God closes doors that we think he should fling wide open. Trusting him when we don't know the full picture can feel difficult, but as we do so more and more we'll build up the muscle memory that makes it easier when we face disappointment. In looking back we see his gentle leading in ways we may not have expected.

Loving Father, thank you for tying me with cords of human kindness.
Keep me safe within your boundaries.

AMY BOUCHER PYE

Return and wait

The Lord has a charge to bring against Judah; he will punish Jacob according to his ways and repay him according to his deeds. In the womb he grasped his brother's heel; as a man he struggled with God. He struggled with the angel and overcame him; he wept and begged for his favour. He found him at Bethel and talked with him there – the Lord God Almighty, the Lord is his name! But you must return to your God; maintain love and justice, and wait for your God always.

As we find ourselves once again in a courtroom scene, God reminds his people of how they were formed. The name of the northern kingdom (which was the name for them all before it split in two), came from the night that Jacob wrestled with God, fighting the angel and vowing that he would not let him go until he blessed him (see Genesis 32:22–32). When God observed Jacob's persistence, he blessed him and renamed him 'Israel', which probably means 'he struggles with God'. Thereafter God's people were called Israel.

But Hosea makes clear that God's people in his day are more like the deceitful Jacob than the patriarch he came to be. According to Bible commentators, in the ancient Near East, being a 'heel-catcher' implied someone was a double-dealer and deceitful (see Genesis 25:26). So when God reminds them of their ancestor, he's not commending them but calling them to repent. He wants them to return to love and justice, to wait for God and his ways.

God's reminder of Jacob comes with a warning – he is calling them to return to him and stop being deceitful – but also the promise of his mercy. Just as he blessed Jacob and changed his name, so too will he welcome his wayward people home. When we repent from our sins – perhaps those of contempt and lies – God runs towards us with open arms, grasping us in his embrace. We can rest and cease our struggles.

Forgiving Father, thank you for promising to release me from my sins. Help me to reach the point of repentance quickly, instead of dithering and delaying. I want to be clean and free.

AMY BOUCHER PYE

Wispy or solid

It is said of these people, 'They offer human sacrifices! They kiss calf-idols!' Therefore they will be like the morning mist, like the early dew that disappears, like chaff swirling from a threshing-floor, like smoke escaping through a window. But I have been the Lord your God ever since you came out of Egypt. You shall acknowledge no God but me, no Saviour except me… When I fed them, they were satisfied; when they were satisfied, they became proud; then they forgot me. So I will be like a lion to them, like a leopard I will lurk by the path. Like a bear robbed of her cubs, I will attack them and rip them open.'

The sins of God's people lead him to despair. The human sacrifices here are probably the hateful practice of child sacrifice – there are not many things more barbaric than that. God pronounces the consequences of their sin, that the people will become as insubstantial as the morning mist or the smoke that escapes out the window.

God then reminds his people how often they forget him when they've found shelter and their bellies are full. To chasten them, he becomes as a lion, a leopard or a bear. These animals were all native predators in the ancient Near East.

In our rush to emphasise repentance and restoration, we may overlook the consequences of sin – our own or that committed against us. Those who refuse to repent may turn into an empty shell of a person; those pumped up with grandiosity and lies may be seen for the hot air they emit. Or they may become so entrenched in their prejudice that grace and mercy will no longer soak into their hardened exterior. Of course, God can work miracles – and he does. But he also respects our choices and won't force himself on us.

We can ask God through his Spirit to keep making us more solid; that as we become more like him we will avoid disappearing as the morning mist. That's a prayer he loves to answer.

Lord, make me solid in you. Fill me with your Spirit that I would act in ways that honour you.

AMY BOUCHER PYE

Trees of Israel

Return, Israel, to the Lord your God. Your sins have been your downfall!… Say to him: 'Forgive all our sins and receive us graciously… Assyria cannot save us; we will not mount war-horses. We will never again say "Our gods" to what our own hands have made'… 'I will heal their waywardness and love them freely, for my anger has turned away from them. I will be like the dew to Israel… Like a cedar of Lebanon he will send down his roots… His splendour will be like an olive tree… People will dwell again in his shade… they will blossom like the vine.'

After the heartache of Hosea taking on a wayward wife, and after the to and fro of the courtroom scene, how refreshing to reach this loving conversation between Hosea on behalf of the people and their God. Hosea calls them to repent, to promise never again to worship the idols they fashion or to trust in the power of armies. God responds with a promise of love in action. He will graciously receive them and will love them without ceasing. He will plant them in good soil; their shoots will grow into a solid tree in whose shade people will find relief from the scorching sun.

We can find hope in this final conversation in the book of Hosea. It affirms that God's nature is to forgive and to restore. Although we fail him, he forgives us. He welcomes us with gentle caresses and loving-kindness. However far we stray – no matter what other idols we worship or if we put our trust into the things we create – he will not cease accepting us.

As you ponder the never-ending love of God through this Old Testament book, consider how you can embody God's loving attributes even more. How can you live out his ways of grace in your intimate relationships? Take some time to converse with God about one particular person, asking him for a revelation that will honour this person and God.

Loving God, make us like a cedar of Lebanon, that others may find relief and comfort in our shade. Help us to grow and flourish, spreading your light and love both near and afar.

AMY BOUCHER PYE

Light and darkness

Christmas is coming! By now houses will be festooned with flashing, twinkling, chasing lights. The long evenings of winter darkness give us plenty of time to appreciate them. Families will wrap up against the cold, don their wellies and set off to spectacular light displays in the grounds of country houses. High Street shopping will be illuminated by giant snowflakes, icicles, stars and ribbons. There won't be much sign of the baby Jesus in all of this, of course. But there will be an abundance of evidence that light shines in the darkness.

In almost every culture darkness is a symbol of evil. It is often under the cover of darkness that wickedness thrives. 'The way of the wicked is like deep darkness' (Proverbs 4:19, NIV). The New Testament refers to the 'works of darkness'. In contrast, 'God is light; in him there is no darkness at all' (1 John 1:5). Darkness is also used as a metaphor for ignorance. My family often think I am in the dark about what is going on! But sometimes the light comes on – and with knowledge comes understanding.

But darkness is not all bad. It was in a dark sky that eastern stargazers saw a star that led them to a king. Sometimes we need the darkness to fully appreciate the light.

We rarely experience the full reality of darkness. Street lights, let alone Christmas illuminations, create a cocoon of light around our towns and cities. People travel to dark-sky discovery sites, where light pollution is low and the glory of the night sky is revealed. I recall being in a remote part of Paraguay, miles from any electric light, and my amazement at seeing the Milky Way splashed vividly across the sky above me.

The baby in the manger grew up to be the one who said, 'I am the light of the world' (John 9:5). As we journey together towards Christmas, day by day, may you have enough illumination to see clearly what God wants to reveal to you from his word. Because Jesus also said, 'You are the world's light… Don't hide your light! Let it shine for all; let your good deeds glow for all to see, so that they will praise your heavenly Father' (Matthew 5:14–16, TLB).

STEPHEN RAND

Let there be light

In the beginning God created the heavens and the earth. Now the earth was formless and empty, darkness was over the surface of the deep, and the Spirit of God was hovering over the waters. And God said, 'Let there be light,' and there was light. God saw that the light was good, and he separated the light from the darkness. God called the light 'day', and the darkness he called 'night'. And there was evening, and there was morning – the first day.

Let's start at the very beginning – a very good place to start! God's creative process began by flooding the darkness of an empty void with light. And 'God saw that the light was good'.

Illumination is still a vital part of the creative process. In a literal sense, intricate craft work is best performed in bright light. In a spiritual sense, the illumination of God's Spirit is essential to the writing of these notes, creating the profound possibility that words typed months ago can impact today's reader with insight, encouragement and challenge.

My wife and I are National Trust volunteers at Waddesdon Manor in Buckinghamshire. One of the stories we love to tell is that Waddesdon was where Queen Victoria first experienced electric light. She was so amazed that the servant had to stand by the switch, turning it on and off, demonstrating the new reality of instant illumination. Human inventiveness had finally replicated this one part of the creative process!

God's creation of day is a constant: it cannot be switched off on a whim. Similarly, God's creative illumination is still always available: to help us find the way forward, to clarify a complex situation. At any moment we can turn to God in prayer and make the request, 'Let there be light!'

Genesis 1 reminds us that God was – and is – the ultimate source of light and life. And the birth of Jesus that we celebrate at Christmas was envisaged right from the start. The incarnation was always part of God's creative plan to reveal himself, his goodness and love; to illuminate the darkness of human sinfulness with the light of the salvation found in Jesus, the light of the world.

Loving Father, bring light into the world's darkness once again.

STEPHEN RAND

The light shines in the darkness

In the beginning was the Word, and the Word was with God, and the Word was God. He was in the beginning with God. All things came into being through him, and without him not one thing came into being. What has come into being in him was life, and the life was the light of all people. The light shines in the darkness, and the darkness did not overcome it.

John's commentary on the Genesis creation story focuses on Jesus, the living Word, the one through whom life – the whole created order – came into being. His gospel doesn't start with a baby in Bethlehem; rather, it begins with a magnificent statement of the cosmic reality and significance of God's plan revealed in Jesus, who 'became flesh and lived among us' (John 1:14).

Scientific textbooks explain that light is essential to life, without it we simply would have nothing. John appears to reverse this: life was the source of light. This is the process of material creation – the light that sustains the life of the planet, and human beings that depend on it, originated with God: Father, Son and Holy Spirit. 'The Word gave life to everything that was created,' says one translation (NLT).

It continues: 'and his life brought light to everyone.' There is so much here! At the simplest level, the life of Jesus illuminates the way life should be lived. I have never been to a life drawing class, either as a sitter or a potential artist – a relief for all concerned! But I know the participants observe closely and replicate the model as closely as they can. Jesus is our model for living. We observe his inclusive love and care, his grace under pressure, his sacrifice for others, and by his Spirit we strive to reproduce these qualities.

Jesus lived his life in a hostile world, surrounded by enemies, those whose position, prestige and way of life were threatened by Jesus' words and actions. They plotted and engineered his death, but could not prevent his resurrection. His light shone in the darkness; those who lived in the darkness may have resisted his light, but they could not snuff it out.

Father, help me to live in your light and to share your light.

STEPHEN RAND

Christmas presence

Where can I go from your Spirit? Where can I flee from your presence?… If I settle on the far side of the sea, even there your hand will guide me, your right hand will hold me fast. If I say, 'Surely the darkness will hide me and the light become night around me,' even the darkness will not be dark to you; the night will shine like the day, for darkness is as light to you. For you created my inmost being; you knit me together in my mother's womb. I praise you because I am fearfully and wonderfully made.

There are those who believe that God created all that exists, but that he is no longer involved: the divine watchmaker, who made his masterpiece, wound it up and left it to run like clockwork.

The psalmist did not share that view. To him God was close and personal, deeply involved with every detail of his life. This began even before his birth, when he was formed in the womb. In fact, the Hebrew word translated 'knit together' is the one used for weaving a fence, so it carries the idea of protection as well as shaping.

That intimacy of relationship continued into his adult life. The God he worshipped was one who guided him, who held him, who was always there for him, wherever he went. There was no escape from his presence, not even darkness could offer a hiding place.

This truth is both reassuring and disconcerting. There are days when we want to hide from God. We may be ashamed of what we have done, or we may be planning to do something we would rather God didn't know about. At that point it may be wise to remember that there is no hiding place; there is no cover of darkness.

There are also days when we feel God is so far away, when life events numb our souls, when we may be overwhelmed with grief. There will be someone reading these words who is dreading Christmas this year, because it will highlight their loss, either through bereavement or broken relationships. But be reassured: God is with you. He does not leave you or forsake you.

Loving Lord, grant me the knowledge of your presence with me
this Christmas.

STEPHEN RAND

All is darkness

So justice is far from us, and righteousness does not reach us. We look for light, but all is darkness; for brightness, but we walk in deep shadows. Like the blind we grope along the wall, feeling our way like people without eyes… So justice is driven back… Truth is nowhere to be found… The Lord looked and was displeased that there was no justice. He saw that there was no one, he was appalled that there was no one to intervene.

Every night the television news reminds us that the world is full of darkness. I remember standing in a school hall in Beslan, Russia, gazing at a wall bearing the photographs of every one of the 186 children who had died when the terrorist siege was ended in September 2004. I remember the chilling dawn chorus of wailing cries of relatives whose loved ones had died of starvation in the cold of the night in Ethiopia in 1984.

There are times when we come face-to-face with the reality of darkness. The statistics of people trafficking, child abuse, domestic abuse, displaced people and so much more are an offence to our minds and a burden on our hearts. Sometimes I try to remember that I am made in the image of God and take some comfort that any pain I feel at human suffering is only a pale reflection of the pain that God must feel.

The danger is that we become immune to the suffering; that we become hard-hearted rather than open-handed in response. In my 30s I returned to the Baptist church I had attended in my 20s. A man who had been a fellow deacon told me that I no longer seemed as angry as I had been. He meant well, but I was deeply concerned. Was I no longer as angry at injustice? Had I settled for comfortable middle-class indifference? Decades later I still want to be angry at what makes God angry.

The prophet Isaiah reminded God's people that God was angry at injustice, appalled that no one cared enough to intervene. So appalled, in fact, that he did intervene, personally. His son was born into the darkness and brought light.

Lord, soften my heart in compassion, and harden my determination to act for truth and justice.

STEPHEN RAND

Release from darkness

The Spirit of the Sovereign Lord is on me, because the Lord has anointed me to proclaim good news to the poor. He has sent me to bind up the broken-hearted, to proclaim freedom for the captives and release from darkness for the prisoners, to proclaim the year of the Lord's favour and the day of vengeance of our God, to comfort all who mourn, and provide for those who grieve in Zion – to bestow on them a crown of beauty instead of ashes, the oil of joy instead of mourning, and a garment of praise instead of a spirit of despair.

Jesus was in his home synagogue, surrounded by his neighbours, those who had known him all his life. He stood up, opened the scroll of the prophet Isaiah and found the verses above. He read the first half of them, then sat down. Everyone waited to hear what he would say: 'Today this scripture is fulfilled in your hearing' (Luke 4:21).

Next, the people of Nazareth were ready to kill him. They understood that the one they knew as Joseph's son was claiming to be the fulfilment of Isaiah's prophecy about the Messiah, the one chosen to deliver Israel.

But the words of the prophet echo down the centuries, a beautiful summary of God's mission invested in his Son. It is rooted in the bitterness of Israel's exile experience – the word translated 'captives' is the word for those carried off into captivity; the release from darkness for the prisoners describes those who come out of the dungeon blinking in the glare of daylight.

In the translation of the Greek New Testament, this has become 'recovery of sight for the blind', a prophecy so readily fulfilled by Jesus healing those born blind. And now? The gospel is still good news to the poor, materially and spiritually. It's all about freedom: freedom to receive his new life and live as God intended – walking in the light.

So why did Jesus stop at the year of the Lord's favour... perhaps that was the message he wanted to emphasise: that his birth, life, death and resurrection were – and are – the greatest sign of all of God's grace, mercy and blessing.

Lord, open my eyes afresh to your good news of freedom.

STEPHEN RAND

New things

This is what God the Lord says – the Creator of the heavens, who stretches them out, who spreads out the earth with all that springs from it, who gives breath to its people, and life to those who walk on it: 'I, the Lord, have called you in righteousness; I will take hold of your hand. I will keep you and will make you to be a covenant for the people and a light for the Gentiles, to open eyes that are blind, to free captives from prison and to release from the dungeon those who sit in darkness… See, the former things have taken place, and new things I declare; before they spring into being I announce them to you.'

As I'm sure you've noticed, today's verses are an echo of yesterday's. This vision of the future clearly mattered to Isaiah. But there is an important difference between the two passages. Yesterday the words were in the first person, describing the life's work of the prophet, an individual empowered by the Spirit of God. Today, the words are directed to a nation, the people of God.

They have been called by God. He promises to guide them ('I will take hold of your hand') and preserve them ('I will keep you'). Why? So that they can be 'a light to the Gentiles'. The Hebrew word translated 'Gentiles' simply means foreign nations, the rest of the world. This is a reworking of the promise to Abraham, that he would be the father of a great nation and that would be a blessing to the world.

God's blessings are never meant to be simply kept and enjoyed: they are always to be shared. Shared with those on the outside, those who are excluded.

The birth of Jesus was seen by Simeon as the coming of the light for the Gentiles (Luke 2:25–35). In the church that came into being after the first Easter, there was no distinction between Jew and Gentile and the good news was taken to the whole world. So this vision becomes a picture of the mission of the church.

God's promise is that he will do new things. What new thing is he calling you and your church to do to bring light and liberation to those currently outside his blessings?

STEPHEN RAND

The triumph of darkness?

From noon until three in the afternoon darkness came over all the land. About three in the afternoon Jesus cried out in a loud voice, '*Eli, Eli, lema sabachthani?*' (which means 'My God, my God, why have you forsaken me?')… And when Jesus had cried out again in a loud voice, he gave up his spirit. At that moment the curtain of the temple was torn in two from top to bottom. The earth shook, the rocks split and the tombs broke open… When the centurion and those with him who were guarding Jesus saw the earthquake and all that had happened, they were terrified, and exclaimed, 'Surely he was the Son of God!'

There is an inextricable link between Christmas and Easter. Mary gazed at the baby in the manger – and around 33 years later watched as her child died on a cross.

Matthew describes two natural phenomena that coincided with the death of Jesus. The first is the onset of darkness at noon. Out of the darkness comes the chilling cry of the separation of Son from Father. I don't pretend to fully understand this moment. But I know that the disciples who had spent three years with Jesus saw it and experienced it as the triumph of darkness, the dashing of all their hopes. The light had been extinguished.

At that moment came the second natural phenomenon: an earthquake that shook the temple so powerfully that the curtain that enclosed the holy of holies was torn wide open. No longer was access to God restricted to the high priest once a year; the death of Jesus opened the way for all to know the presence of God for themselves. The earthquake also broke open the tombs – a symbolic revelation that the death of Jesus brings new life.

Matthew records one other miracle. The Roman centurion in charge of the execution squad watched Jesus die and saw something that prompted his remarkable exclamation. He was the first of millions of other 'outsiders' who would recognise Jesus as the Son of God. As Jesus died in the darkness, he was indeed a light to the Gentiles.

Praise you, Lord: 'Death defeated, life vindicated in a steady blaze of light, all through the work of Jesus' (2 Timothy 1:10, MSG)

STEPHEN RAND

Consequences

This is the message we have heard from him and declare to you: God is light; in him there is no darkness at all. If we claim to have fellowship with him and yet walk in the darkness, we lie and do not live out the truth. But if we walk in the light, as he is in the light, we have fellowship with one another, and the blood of Jesus, his Son, purifies us from all sin.

I'm old enough to remember the tradition of playing parlour games at Christmas – my children are still slightly traumatised by one of my more flamboyant charade performances when they were young and impressionable. It's a lifetime since I played 'consequences': each player has a sheet of paper, and all are told to write down a word or phrase to fit a description, then, folding the paper over to hide what they've written, they hand it to the next person. This is repeated several times so that each piece of paper contains a very random story. The final line always must answer the question – 'And the consequence was…?'

When we decide to follow Jesus, there are consequences. As John expresses it here, we have fellowship with God and we have fellowship with one another. Isn't it truly amazing that we can be linked to God, we can walk with him and talk with him, all because of what Jesus has done? Sometimes we find it slightly less amazing that we are linked to our fellow Christians. What a bunch they are! And if you feel like that about them, imagine how they feel about you!

Yet John is making a serious point. Our actions must be consistent with our convictions. God is light; there is no room for any compromise with darkness. Every time I say I love God and decide to please myself, I am living a lie.

So we are instructed and challenged to 'walk in the light'. When we do, God himself will illuminate our decision-making and the way ahead will be clear. And the consequence will be that we'll enjoy sharing the journey with others and our whole being will be cleaned out and made pure by Jesus.

Father, help me to walk in the light each day.

STEPHEN RAND

Blinded by the light

'On one of these journeys I was going to Damascus with the authority and commission of the chief priests. About noon… I saw a light from heaven, brighter than the sun… I heard a voice saying to me in Aramaic, "Saul, Saul, why do you persecute me?"… Then I asked, "Who are you, Lord?" "I am Jesus, whom you are persecuting," the Lord replied… "I am sending you to them to open their eyes and turn them from darkness to light, and from the power of Satan to God, so that they may receive forgiveness of sins and a place among those who are sanctified by faith in me."'

As we look back at the history of the church from our particular vantage point, it could be said that we can trace our family tree of faith back to one moment: when Saul met Jesus on the road to Damascus. His name was changed, his whole life was changed. He became Paul, the great missionary to the non-Jewish world. The churches he established were the basis of the spread of the church across the Roman Empire – including a cold and hostile island off the coast of Gaul. And that island, Britain, became the home of another great missionary movement across the globe hundreds of years later.

Saul's journey was interrupted by a blinding light and the voice of Jesus, which commissioned him to the task of turning people from darkness to light, of opening the eyes of others to the reality of the risen Jesus he had now met for himself. This encounter shaped his understanding of the gospel; he became a man on a mission.

One last thought: Paul's missionary journeys replaced his persecution journeys. He encountered Jesus as he was on his way to hunt down Christians in a bid to crush the church before it could take root. As we approach Christmas, there are fellow Christians, our sisters and brothers, who still fear the knock on the door, who dread the arrival of the secret police or the angry mob determined to hunt them down and destroy the church. Christmas can be a particularly dangerous time.

Father, we pray that those intent on persecuting your people this Christmas might have a life-changing encounter with Jesus.

STEPHEN RAND

His light shines in our hearts

The god of this age has blinded the minds of unbelievers, so that they cannot see the light of the gospel that displays the glory of Christ, who is the image of God. For what we preach is not ourselves, but Jesus Christ as Lord, and ourselves as your servants for Jesus' sake. For God, who said, 'Let light shine out of darkness,' made his light shine in our hearts to give us the light of the knowledge of God's glory displayed in the face of Christ.

It's clear just how much Paul's experience on the Damascus road influenced his understanding of the gospel. He had been arrested by a blinding light: the good news of the new life to be found in Jesus would always for him be associated with light. As we've seen, this was not a new thought. But what had been an interesting viewpoint of Jewish theology was now seared into his psyche and central to his teaching.

The light hadn't just shone in his eyes; God had made his light shine in his heart. Paul was steeped in Jewish understanding. To him, the heart was the centre of an individual's thought, emotions and spiritual life. Jesus was the illumination of his entire thinking, all his mental processes. The letters he wrote to the churches he established are full of the deepest theological concepts; it is Paul's intelligence that moulded Christian theology forever, informed by the 'light of the knowledge of God's glory'.

But these verses are not dominated by knowledge. They radiate with light, and that light is God's glory 'displayed in the face of Christ'. Paul's intelligence explored the meaning of his encounter of Christ; his memory of it was overwhelmed with glory. My guess is that he understood, at that moment, why Moses had not been allowed to see the face of God.

Nowadays, mention Christianity and so many people just can't see it; as Paul puts it here, their minds are blinded. I'm sure one reason is simply that God's people don't always display 'the glory of Christ'. If his followers revealed more of Jesus in the grace of their talking and the love of their actions, people might be more open-minded about him.

Lord, may my life reflect your glory.

STEPHEN RAND

Don't stop praying

Since the day we heard about you, we have not stopped praying for you. We continually ask God to fill you with the knowledge of his will through all the wisdom and understanding that the Spirit gives, so that you may live a life worthy of the Lord and please him in every way: bearing fruit... and giving joyful thanks to the Father, who has qualified you to share in the inheritance of his holy people in the kingdom of light. For he has rescued us from the dominion of darkness and brought us into the kingdom of the Son he loves, in whom we have redemption, the forgiveness of sins.

Paul cared so much about the people in the churches he had initiated that he prayed for them regularly. Many years ago, I highlighted in these notes my debt to the folk in the church where I grew up who had prayed for me every day since I was a small boy. When they had been published, a friend read them out during the morning service and at least one of my faithful prayer supporters heard of my appreciation. She died a short while after this; I felt that God had moved in a mysterious way to ensure that she knew her vital ministry was not forgotten.

I love this prayer of Paul's. It starts by focusing on the consequences we thought about earlier. He is asking God to fill them with knowledge, wisdom and understanding. Why? So they can live lives that honour God and bear fruit. As a missionary Paul had made sure that the light of the gospel had been taken to the Gentiles; that light had to continue to shine in and through the Christian community so that more would be drawn to the light, receive forgiveness and new life... and so the church would grow.

His words underline the seriousness of the mission: 'rescued'; 'redemption'; 'forgiveness'. Following Jesus meant a change of citizenship, from the dominion of darkness to the kingdom of light. Paul prayed with thanks for those who had changed their passport in this way and prayed that many more would do the same.

---

*Pause now: pray for someone you care about, using the words
in the second sentence of today's verses.*

STEPHEN RAND

The family at Christmas

This old command is the message you have heard. Yet I am writing you a new command; its truth is seen in him and in you, because the darkness is passing and the true light is already shining. Anyone who claims to be in the light but hates a brother or sister is still in the darkness. Anyone who loves their brother and sister lives in the light, and there is nothing in them to make them stumble. But anyone who hates a brother or sister is in the darkness and walks around in the darkness. They do not know where they are going, because the darkness has blinded them.

Are you dreading Christmas Day? The day when we can remember the moment that God intervened decisively in human history by being born as a baby is for many overshadowed by the stress of the family get-together. Some find their in-laws or their own parents difficult to be with. Thankfully this is not everyone's experience, but sadly it is for many.

In today's verses John talks about hating a brother or sister. He's not thinking of siblings fighting over a Christmas present. He is focused on the family of God, our fellow Christians. In his gospel he had recorded the prayer of Jesus, that his followers might 'be one as we are one' (John 17:22). He had quoted Jesus saying, 'By this everyone will know that you are my disciples, if you love one another' (John 13:35). John was deeply convinced that the behaviour of Christians towards one another was key to people being convinced of the truth of the gospel.

John's gospel and his letters are full of references to God's love, expressed in Jesus – he loved the world so much he gave his Son. And the followers of Jesus should behave like Jesus. 'This is how we know what love is: Jesus Christ laid down his life for us. And we ought to lay down our lives for our brothers and sisters' (1 John 3:16). What a challenge!

If you are able to be in church over this Christmas period take a look at your fellow worshippers and remember: Jesus was born because God loves you – and so you would love them.

STEPHEN RAND

To us a child is born

The people walking in darkness have seen a great light; on those living in the land of deep darkness a light has dawned… You have shattered the yoke that burdens them, the bar across their shoulders, the rod of their oppressor… For to us a child is born, to us a son is given, and the government will be on his shoulders. And he will be called Wonderful Counsellor, Mighty God, Everlasting Father, Prince of Peace. Of the greatness of his government and peace there will be no end. He will reign on David's throne and over his kingdom, establishing and upholding it with justice and righteousness from that time on and forever.

This is one of the great Bible readings in the Festival of Nine Lessons and Carols, and it is a highlight of Handel's *Messiah*. Christians are convinced that Isaiah's prophetic words were fulfilled in the birth of Jesus. It's not difficult to see why!

It is a glittering trumpet fanfare of hope, full of excitement and conviction about the future. There is a light at the end of the tunnel of gloom and despair. Slaves will be liberated, the oppressor banished. There will be a new order, characterised by peace and justice. And the agent of this triumphant change will be a child, a son that will carry the name of God the Father and the Holy Spirit.

It was a vision of hope for God's people in Isaiah's day, a promise of a king who would be everything a king should be. The king would have an extraordinary name that would describe God himself, the one who will work in and through the king to fulfil this vision. The name may be best translated, 'A Wonderful Counsellor is the Mighty God, the Everlasting Father is a Prince of Peace.'

The vision is yet to be fulfilled, and while the New Testament does not specifically say that Jesus is the fulfilment of this particular prophecy, it is very clear that the birth of Jesus *is* an indication that God is fulfilling his purposes. He has not given up on his promise that the kingdom of peace and justice will one day be established.

Everlasting Father, this Christmas renew my hope and grant your peace.

STEPHEN RAND

Glory in the darkness

And there were shepherds living out in the fields near by, keeping watch over their flocks at night. An angel of the Lord appeared to them, and the glory of the Lord shone around them, and they were terrified. But the angel said to them, 'Do not be afraid. I bring you good news that will cause great joy for all the people. Today in the town of David a Saviour has been born to you; he is the Messiah, the Lord. This will be a sign to you: you will find a baby wrapped in cloths and lying in a manger.' Suddenly a great company of the heavenly host appeared with the angel, praising God and saying, 'Glory to God in the highest heaven, and on earth peace…'

The darkness exploded into light! No wonder the shepherds were terrified. They were used to the quiet loneliness of their nocturnal existence; they had no warning of the celestial firework display that announced the turning point in human history. They may have been relieved that it began with only one angel opening the door from heaven and allowing God's glory to come flooding out to shine around them. The great company of angels provided a wonderful choral finale.

Glory in the darkness was not the only contrast that night. The shepherds came face to face with the heavenly host. The greatest breaking news bulletin of all time was delivered, exclusively, to hired labourers considered so untrustworthy that their evidence was discounted in the courts.

But then over history the good news of Jesus has always tended to bring great joy to the poor, the excluded, the oppressed, the disenfranchised. The most enthusiastic worship I ever experienced was in a ramshackle refugee camp church packed with people who had fled from violence and wondered if they would ever return home. The Jesus they worshipped had shared their experience: born in a makeshift shelter far from home, soon to become a refugee to escape terror.

That Christmas night the glory of heaven lit up a remote corner of the world. Praise God that it still does.

The birth of Jesus gave glory to God in heaven and promised peace on earth – we long for that promise to be fulfilled.

STEPHEN RAND

For my eyes have seen

Now there was a man in Jerusalem called Simeon, who was righteous and devout. He was waiting for the consolation of Israel, and the Holy Spirit was on him... When the parents brought in the child Jesus... Simeon took him in his arms and praised God, saying: 'Sovereign Lord, as you have promised, you may now dismiss your servant in peace. For my eyes have seen your salvation, which you have prepared in the sight of all nations: a light for revelation to the Gentiles, and the glory of your people Israel.'

Merry Christmas. For the children, the waiting will soon be over, if not already. Wrapping paper will be all over the floor, and presents that will delight (hopefully) will be gazed at with excitement, perhaps even wonder (not as in 'I wonder why they gave me this...').

Simeon had been waiting. And when he took Jesus in his arms, there was excitement and wonder that provoked praise to God, the giver of the gift of a tiny baby. These are great verses for an old man like me. I treasure the memory of when, on the day she was born, our youngest grandchild Stella Hope was in my arms for the first time. Simeon, almost certainly old, looked down and saw more than a baby. He saw a vital step in God's plan of salvation, a plan that encompassed the whole world: 'A light for revelation to the Gentiles, and the glory of your people Israel.'

I love the old masters' interpretations of the manger – you may have examples on your Christmas cards. While they may lack biblical and historical accuracy (Donkeys? Wise men and shepherds together?) they often demonstrate theological understanding. For the illumination of the whole stable often emanates directly from the baby Jesus: he illuminates the painting, because he is the light of salvation revealed to the whole world.

You may not have much opportunity in the busyness of Christmas Day, but just take a moment, close your eyes, imagine holding a baby in your arms. And share in the joy of Simeon, because your eyes have seen the light of your salvation.

Today, Christmas Day, let me share in Simeon's joy, and know the peace for which he longed.

STEPHEN RAND

Beyond Christmas

By the time we reach Christmas we have been listening to – or at least hearing – Christmas carols for at least a month. As the turkey leftovers and recycled brussels sprouts are eaten up or thrown away, so too are the carols put back in their box, to be silenced for another eleven months. Strictly speaking, we should not sing Christmas carols until after Christmas Eve, the period preceding being Advent, when we prepare for Christmas. Yet musically, we pre-empt the great celebration, which means that having consumed a great deal before Christmas we soon abandon them from well before the twelfth day of Christmas.

This Christmas, let's continue to digest some of those carols, for trivial they are not and mostly biblical they are. Let us look under the bonnet of some of our carols to see the scripture on which they stand and the ever-relevant message of peace, goodwill and joy which they bring, and the Emmanuel – God with us – whom they herald.

Every Christmas carol has its own story, and often a salvation story to tell too. It has a tale of its own which can be fascinating, surprising, even shocking. Some Christmas carols are not what they seem to be. There are many books telling the stories of Christmas carols, and some of them are even based on fact. Others see carols as part of the folklore of Christmas, the musical equivalent of cranberry sauce or brandy butter, a bitter sweetener or rich embellishment to disguise the real flavour, or indeed make it taste of something else. As Christians we want to see, hear, smell, taste and see Christmas, so it sounds, looks and feels like Christmas, even in the face of the fairy-tale version, to which 'Away in a Manger' and 'Jingle Bells' are the soundtrack.

Many Christmas carols are hymns, praising God and telling the story, often in the form of a paraphrase. You have been listening to them for a month now. So, come, all ye faithful, and let's take a look at them together. Let's look as well as listen, that we may see the glory of God and hear the angels' song afresh, even as Christmas recedes and we are drawn away from the Big Day further into the Christmas season.

GORDON GILES

On the feast of Stephen

Now during those days, when the disciples were increasing in number, the Hellenists complained against the Hebrews because their widows were being neglected in the daily distribution of food. And the twelve… chose Stephen, a man full of faith and the Holy Spirit… Stephen, full of grace and power, did great wonders and signs among the people.

'Good King Wenceslas looked out, on the feast of Stephen…' Boxing Day has its own unique carol, written by the prolific hymn-translator John Mason Neale in 1853. The Victorian approach to Christmas had by then already taken root: Prince Albert's Christmas tree arrived in 1841 and Dickens' *A Christmas Carol* was published in December 1843. Thus the 'goodwill to all' message of the angels was translated to an industrial society in which the rich were very rich and the poor very poor. The Christian's duty was to not only turn the nativity of Jesus into a true 'feast' day, but to remember the poor, if only for a day or two. Dickens encouraged it and Neale blessed those who did at the end of his carol, which mentions Stephen but not Jesus. Their legacy is very much still with us, and it's almost unbelievable that Christmas was barely observed before the mid-19th century.

Yet Boxing Day is not the day for charity because Good King Wenceslas says so. Rather, it is because it is the day we commemorate the first Christian martyr, Stephen, who was lynched in the presence of Paul. It was Stephen who was appointed to the servant (diaconal) role of ministering to the poor and hungry. Since Christmas is a time of gifts, it is worth noticing that – although Ebenezer Scrooge gave a gift of a turkey to the Cratchit family, the magi brought gifts to the crib and indeed Christ is God's gift to the world – in Stephen we are reminded of a recurring, personal gift: the gift we have in the call to service. For in receiving the gift of Christian service with which we can serve our neighbours, we receive a great blessing.

Or, as Neale put it, 'Therefore, Christian men, be sure, wealth or rank possessing, Ye who now will bless the poor, shall yourselves find blessing.'

How can you use the gift of Christian service?

GORDON GILES

God of God

In the beginning was the Word, and the Word was with God, and the Word was God. He was in the beginning with God. All things came into being through him, and without him not one thing came into being. What has come into being in him was life, and the life was the light of all people. The light shines in the darkness, and the darkness did not overcome it…. And the Word became flesh and lived among us, and we have seen his glory.

'O come, all ye faithful…' This carol gives us the full Christmas works. It presents the story of Christmas with verses about shepherds and magi, but also contains direct reference to John 1. The final verse is often only sung on Christmas Day, which makes it very special. When the gathered faithful sing, 'Yea, Lord, we greet thee, born this happy morning', Christmas has arrived, Christ is born anew in our hearts and the full range of Christmas gifts, including the calling to Christian service, come into play.

Known to some as *Adeste Fideles*, the hymn was originally written in Latin, as the author, John Francis Wade, was a Jacobite, a Catholic seeking the restoration of the Stuart monarchy, through a French-assisted invasion of Britain to put Bonnie Prince Charlie on the throne. The mere fact that the hymn, telling the story of incarnation as described by John, is in Latin was a political statement and a call to supporters (the 'faithful') to rally to the rightful heir, in opposition to Protestant rule.

This rarely occurs to us when we sing 'O come, all ye faithful' now, nor should it. First-century history prevails over politics, and we are left with the truth that is both simple and complex: that God came and dwelt among us, one of us, God of God and light of light, begotten, not created. And in that unique and miraculous event is the meaning of life, the forgiveness of sins and the glory of God, proclaimed by choirs of angels.

'Word of the Father, now in flesh appearing.
O come let us adore him… Christ the Lord.'
How can you adore the Word made flesh
and light of the world in these dark days?

GORDON GILES

Wholly innocent

When Herod saw that he had been tricked by the wise men, he was infuriated, and he sent and killed all the children in and around Bethlehem who were two years old or under, according to the time that he had learned from the wise men. Then was fulfilled what had been spoken through the prophet Jeremiah: 'A voice was heard in Ramah, wailing and loud lamentation, Rachel weeping for her children; she refused to be consoled, because they are no more.'

Holy Innocents' Day is one of the toughest days in the liturgical calendar, and because it falls in the post-Christmas period it is often overlooked. In recent years, when the physical, sexual, mental or emotional abuse of children has been so much in the news, the 'massacre of the innocents' takes on modern overtones. Herod abused children; but he was not the first to do so, and even those who are caught doing it tomorrow will not be the last. What is it in human nature that leads to such barbaric violence against the wholly innocent?

Stories like this remind us that sin is real and that anyone who thinks sin is an old-fashioned concept, or something with which to subdue the faithful, is as misguided and deluded as Herod was.

The Coventry Carol, first catalogued by the Pageant of the Shearmen and Tailors of that city in the 14th century, makes a musical bouquet of Rachel's lamentation, and in the sheer beauty of simplicity tears at the heart strings as a lullaby becomes a lament. Set within its proper context of the dramatised mystery plays, it is a deeply poignant but not sentimental carol which exposes the dark underbelly of the Christmas story, with its evil intent, insecurity and abuse personified in Herod. It also connects birth and death (as does the story of Stephen two days ago), reminding us that even though the baby Jesus escapes the horrors of despotic infanticide, others died in his place, and his destiny is to die for others. His death, like his birth, is unique, and is for all his children, of any age, in any age.

'Herod the king, in his raging, Chargèd he hath this day,
His men of might in his own sight, All young children to slay.'
Safeguarding of children is for everyone: what part can you play?

GORDON GILES

Guiding star

In the time of King Herod, after Jesus was born in Bethlehem of Judea, wise men from the East came to Jerusalem, asking, 'Where is the child who has been born king of the Jews? For we observed his star at its rising, and have come to pay him homage'… They set out; and there, ahead of them, went the star that they had seen at its rising, until it stopped over the place where the child was. When they saw that the star had stopped, they were overwhelmed with joy.

'As with gladness, men of old, did the guiding star behold…' Sometimes sung at carol services, William Chatterton Dix's hymn was written on 6 January 1859, when he was too ill in bed to go to church, so had to stay at home for the Epiphany service. Although there are debates annually about how you count the twelve days of Christmas or when 'Twelfth Night' is, Epiphany focuses on the revealing of Christ to the Gentiles and on the wise men and their gifts. Dix knew this, so it is ironic that his Epiphany hymn is now considered to be a Christmas carol. For Epiphany means 'revealing' and Christ can be revealed any day, and we can always celebrate and recognise that.

The story of the magi is lit both by the stars and divine light. Guided by a divine night light, the group of magi went on a pilgrimage to find the true light of light, who came into being, like the stars, at the beginning of time. In the story of the magi, the Big Bang of creation and the explosion of divine love that is the incarnation connect and cross, and Jesus' story – his story – cuts across the history of the universe.

The questing magi are like us, and Dix's glowing words lift us from the annual Christmas journey through the cold turkey leftovers and stale pudding, to the warmth of eternal light that beckons us all on our earthly pilgrimage to eternal knowledge and salvation and beyond. For as Dix concludes, 'As with joy they hailed its light, leading onward, beaming bright, so, most gracious God, may we, evermore be led to thee.'

Where are you in your earthly pilgrimage? Can you see the light?

GORDON GILES

What child is this?

After eight days had passed, it was time to circumcise the child; and he was called Jesus, the name given by the angel before he was conceived in the womb.

'What child is this, who, laid to rest on Mary's lap, is sleeping?' William Chatterton Dix, who wrote 'As With Gladness' (see yesterday's reflection) also wrote this equally profound carol, repeatedly asking, 'Who is Jesus?' We could say, 'It is Jesus, named on the eighth day according to Jewish tradition, according to the instruction given to Mary by Gabriel.' Yet each of us should ask and answer for ourselves. Each Christmas this question cuts through the cake and soaks up the pudding: who, what, how is Jesus? This baby on the lap of Mary, looking and crying and seeming like any other child, but who has been born amid animals, been sought by shepherds, survived a murder attempt and been found by foreigners who bring him dazzling and meaningful gifts – who *is* this?

'This, this is Christ the King, whom shepherds worship and angels sing.' But also as the carol reminds us, 'Nails, spear shall pierce him through, the cross be borne for me, for you.' This silent, sleeping child, though he be the son of Mary, is the Word made flesh. The ever-so-human baby's birth has theological meaning which causes us, with furrowed brow, to ask, 'What child is this?'

As Christmas recedes, we can stick to the sentimental, shallow answers or we can peer deeper, attempting to really explore the significance of the Word made flesh, of Christ our king, and the way in which the human baby son of Mary can be both of these. While the choice is ours, we can never avoid the sense that there is more than humanity being described by Luke. And if we can grasp the dual nature of this human-divine child, asleep in Mary's arms, but also wake up to the sin of the world, we can remember that Jesus is the same yesterday, today and tomorrow, and it is his name which every tongue shall confess and before whom all knees shall bow: 'All tongues and peoples own him, the King of kings salvation brings, let every heart enthrone him.'

Who is Jesus in your heart and mind?

GORDON GILES

Thanks for all that is to be

'Master, now you are dismissing your servant in peace, according to your word; for my eyes have seen your salvation, which you have prepared in the presence of all peoples, a light for revelation to the Gentiles and for glory to your people Israel'… When they had finished … they returned to Galilee, to their own town of Nazareth.

There is a wonderful hymn to sing at the end of a year, by Bishop Timothy Dudley-Smith, entitled 'O Christ the same, through all our story's pages'. The past few years have not been easy, and as we have turned the pages at the end of 2020, 2021 and now 2022, we have had mixed emotions – hopes and fears for all those years. As 2022 departs, we might pray the words of old faithful Simeon. May 2022 depart in peace. And may we say farewell to it in the same way we face our own ultimate departure, with a glimpse of glory and a sense of salvation.

'O Christ the same' is suitable for weddings and for the turn of the year. Its three verses are sung to the famous Irish tune, the 'Londonderry Air (Danny Boy)'. The key to its powerful, profound poetry is the final line of each verse. The first verse looks back over 'passing years' and concludes: 'O Christ the same, who wrought our whole salvation, we bring our thanks for all our yesterdays.' So we thank God for the departing past.

The final line of the central verse is: 'O Christ the same, to whom our hearts are given, we bring our thanks for this, the present hour.' Thus we thank God for *now* – the boundary of past and future, this moment in which we live and move and have our being.

The final verse begins: 'O Christ the same, secure within whose keeping our lives and loves, our days and years remain.' And it concludes: 'O Christ the same, beyond our brief tomorrows, we bring our thanks for all that is to be.' To thank God for those as yet unreceived gifts, the assurance of the unseen, to welcome uncertain futures which lie in God's merciful hands, is faith in word and deed.

Can you thank God for last year, this year and next year?

GORDON GILES

Become a Friend of BRF
and give regularly to support our ministry

We help people of all ages to grow in faith

We encourage and support individual Christians and churches as they
serve and resource the changing spiritual needs of communities today.

Through **Anna Chaplaincy**
we're enabling churches to provide
spiritual care to older people

Through **Living Faith**
we're nurturing faith and resourcing
life-long discipleship

Through **Messy Church**
we're helping churches to reach out
to families

Through **Parenting for Faith**
we're supporting parents as they raise
their children in the Christian faith

Our ministry is only possible because of the generous support of
individuals, churches, trusts and gifts in wills.

As we look to the future and make plans, **regular donations make a
huge difference** in ensuring we can both start and finish projects well.

By becoming a Friend of BRF and giving regularly to our ministry you are
partnering with us in the gospel and helping change lives.

How your gift makes a difference

£2 a month — Helps us to develop **Living Faith** resources to use in care homes and communities

£10 a month — Helps us to support churches running the **Parenting for Faith** course and stand alongside parents

£5 a month — Helps us to support **Messy Church** volunteers and resource and grow the wider network

£20 a month — Helps us to resource **Anna Chaplaincy** and improve spiritual care for older people

How to become a Friend of BRF

Set up a Direct Debit donation at **brf.org.uk/donate** or find out how to set up a Standing Order at **brf.org.uk/friends**

Contact the fundraising team

Email: **giving@brf.org.uk**
Tel: +44 (0)1235 462305
Post: Fundraising team, BRF, 15 The Chambers,
            Vineyard, Abingdon OX14 3FE

Good to know

If you have any questions, or if you want to change your regular donation or stop giving in the future, do get in touch.

Registered with

FUNDRAISING
REGULATOR

SHARING OUR VISION – MAKING A ONE-OFF GIFT

I would like to make a donation to support BRF.
Please use my gift for:

☐ Where it is most needed ☐ Anna Chaplaincy ☐ Living Faith

☐ Messy Church ☐ Parenting for Faith

Title	First name/initials	Surname

Address		

		Postcode

Email		

Telephone		

Signature		Date

Our ministry is only possible because of the generous support of individuals, churches, trusts and gifts in wills.

giftaid it   You can add an extra 25p to every £1 you give.

Please treat as Gift Aid donations all qualifying gifts of money made

☐ today,   ☐ in the past four years,   ☐ and in the future.

I am a UK taxpayer and understand that if I pay less Income Tax and/or Capital Gains Tax in the current tax year than the amount of Gift Aid claimed on all my donations, it is my responsibility to pay any difference.

☐ My donation does not qualify for Gift Aid.

Please notify BRF if you want to cancel this Gift Aid declaration, change your name or home address, or no longer pay sufficient tax on your income and/or capital gains.

Please complete other side of form

SHARING OUR VISION – MAKING A ONE-OFF GIFT

Please accept my gift of:

☐ £2 ☐ £5 ☐ £10 ☐ £20 Other £ [   ]

by (*delete as appropriate*):

☐ Cheque/Charity Voucher payable to 'BRF'

☐ MasterCard/Visa/Debit card/Charity card

Name on card

Card no. [ ][ ][ ][ ] [ ][ ][ ][ ] [ ][ ][ ][ ] [ ][ ][ ][ ]

Expires end [M][M] [Y][Y] Security code* [ ][ ][ ]

*Last 3 digits on the reverse of the card
ESSENTIAL IN ORDER TO PROCESS
YOUR PAYMENT

Signature   Date

☐ I would like to leave a gift to BRF in my will.
  Please send me further information.

For help or advice regarding making a gift, please contact
our fundraising team +44 (0)1865 462305

Your privacy

We will use your personal data to process this transaction.
From time to time we may send you information about
the work of BRF that we think may be of interest to you.
Our privacy policy is available at **brf.org.uk/privacy**.
Please contact us if you wish to discuss your mailing
preferences.

Registered with

 Please complete other side of form

Please return this form to 'Freepost BRF'
No other address information or stamp is needed

Bible Reading Fellowship is a charity (233280) and company limited by
guarantee (301324), registered in England and Wales

Overleaf... Reading *New Daylight* in a group | Author profile | Recommended reading | Order and subscription forms

Reading *New Daylight* in a group

GORDON GILES

In the Rule of Benedict, which formed the spiritual foundations of the daily prayer life of so many ecclesiastical foundations, daily reading was a key aspect of the community life of work and prayer. The distinct disciplines of reading scripture alone and reading together were both significant in the spiritual and moral formation of monks of every rank. With these daily Bible notes we offer scripture and reflective material for personal reading. Yet discussion or shared reflection on the passages chosen and the comments made can also be rewarding, so we offer some 'open' questions that may enable discussion in a Bible study or other group who gather to take further what is published here. The same questions may aid personal devotion too. Use them as you wish, and may God bless and inspire you on your journey as you read holy words and ponder them in your heart.

General discussion starters

These can be used for any study series within this issue. Remember there are no right or wrong answers – these questions are simply to enable a group to engage in conversation.

- What do you think is the main idea or theme of the author in this series? Did that come across strongly?

- Have any of the issues discussed touched on personal – or shared – specifics of your life?

- What evidence or stories do the authors draw on to illuminate, or be illuminated by, the passages of scripture?

- Which do you prefer: scripture informing daily modern life, or modern life shining a new light on scripture?

- Does the author 'call you to action' in a realistic and achievable way? Do you think their ideas will work in the secular world?

- Have any specific passages struck you personally? If so, how and why? Is God speaking to you through scripture and reflection?

- Was anything completely new to you? Were there any 'eureka' or jaw-dropping moments? If so, what difference will that make?

Questions for specific series

Looking forward (Gordon Giles)

- How easy is it to relate to those places spiritually and mentally? Is the past a foreign country or does the Holy Spirit give us a passport to the presence of the past?

- What places today remind you of the churches John writes to? Which do you recognise most readily? Where, if at all, does your church community, and your personal faith, fit in with the seven churches?

Unfamiliar voices of the New Testament (Sally Welch)

- How many of the voices were familiar to you? Were any of them unknown? Share and reflect on what you learned about them.

- Compare and contrast some of the voices (e.g. Jairus' daughter and Pilate's wife; the lawyer and the tomb guards; Simon the tanner and Simon the sorcerer) and the significance of each in the eyes of God.

- Is there anything these unfamiliar human beings, as bit parts in the divine drama, have in common? (The clue is in the question!)

Light and darkness (Stephen Rand)

- Are you still in 'Advent mode' by mid-December? Or have you moved into 'the run up to Christmas'? What does it mean for God to be both 'a present' and 'present' at Christmas?

- The last two Decembers – 2020 and 2021 – were darkened by Covid-19. How were your last two Christmases? How will this year be different? What are your hopes and fears for the end of this year?

- How important are family gatherings and other parties at Christmas? Why ? Is Christmas each year a destination or a journey of sorts?

Holy Habits: Fellowship (Michael Mitton)

Life Together is well worth reading, if you can. How can one be 'alone' in a group, in a positive way, or feel connected to others when alone? Is discussing scripture together part of 'life together'? In recent years how has the idea of 'being alone' been changed or affected?

Meet the author: Sally Welch

Tell us about your church context.

I am vicar of a small town in the Cotswolds. Apart from six years in Oxford, my ministry has always been within the rural church, and I have a deep love for the landscape and people of the countryside. I only have one main church, so administration and meetings can be kept to a minimum. The people of this parish are warm-hearted and generous, actively involved in the community as well as within the church, and it is a joy to serve them.

How did you find being editor of *New Daylight*, and how does it feel now you have handed it over?

I was editor for seven years and found the experience challenging, interesting, moving and exacting – but above all a real privilege. Sometimes, reading through a fortnight's set of notes in one go, I was moved to tears by the content. At others, I have been led to see a familiar passage in a completely new way. *New Daylight* has informed my sermon writing, developed my scriptural knowledge and led me in preciously undiscovered pathways of understanding and deepening of faith. I will always be grateful to BRF for giving me the opportunity to edit such a significant and useful publication.

What have you been doing recently?

My latest book is the second of a twin set called 'Sharing the Story'. The BRF Lent book for 2022 was *Sharing the Easter Story*, and this is partnered by *Sharing the Christmas Story*, the BRF Advent book (see next page). Both explore how individuals, groups and communities can share the wonderful story of Christ's birth, death and resurrection, and what it means for all people, through a process of listening, understanding, living and finally sharing the gospel with those around them.

How has Covid affected you and your community?

My abiding memories of living through Covid are of trying to enable our community to gather and worship God and to serve our neighbours. I spent hours trying to implement government and church guidance, wrestled with new technology, distributed food parcels to the isolated and vulnerable, and supplied 'worship at home' material to those who wanted it. I have also moved hundreds of chairs into many different configurations, thanking the former incumbent who oversaw the re-ordering of the church to bring a vital flexibility to the fixtures and fittings of the building!

Recommended reading

In this year's BRF Advent book Sally Welch explores two questions: What is the Christmas story really about, and how do we share it? Through each week of Advent, a different aspect of the Christmas story is examined: light, promise, mystery, love, peace and hope. Within each week, the days are focused on the ways in which the Christmas story is shared: prophecies, journeys, new life, signs, poems, stories and conversations. Each day offers a Bible passage, followed by a reflection and prayer activity. Suggestions for group study and group study questions are also included.

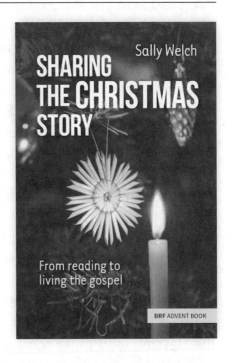

One hundred years ago, in 1922, at a church in south London, the Fellowship of St Matthew was begun in response to a congregation's eagerness for informed and helpful support in building a habit of daily Bible reading. In 1926, it became known as the Bible Reading Fellowship (BRF) as its influence spread and more and more church communities subscribed to the notes and prayers which were offered.

Today, BRF resources people and groups as they grow in faith, encouraging them to deepen their relationship with God and to share the good news of Jesus Christ with others.

These Advent reflections are written in response to BRF's vision of 'Sharing the Story', by looking at the events surrounding the birth of the Messiah. They will take you on a journey through familiar and unfamiliar parts of the Bible, reading and reflecting on our Christian faith.

This journey does not involve a traditional, chronological approach but rather explores each week one of the themes of Advent and Christmas. Beginning with God's promises, shared with us by the prophets throughout the Old Testament, we see how the incarnation is the fulfilment of all those promises. The 'light of the world' has descended from heaven to live among us, and we explore the nature of that light and of all that it has brought to those who live in the darkness of fear, sickness or mourning. Our explorations will not take us far, however, before we engage in the mystery of the overshadowing of Mary by the Holy Spirit and the wonderful complexity of Jesus Christ, fully divine and fully human. However, the love which surrounds us, offering us healing and comfort, support and encouragement is made real at the moment of birth – something we can trust in and depend upon when the challenges of life threaten to overwhelm us.

In Week 5, the issues which surround the nature of peace are engaged with as we both recognise the gap between the 'now and the not yet' and celebrate the gift of peace which Christ's life, death and resurrection make available to us. Finally, we look forward in hope to all that Christ's birth brings to humanity and the final reconciliation which will take place in heaven and on earth.

Each of these themes is explored through a daily focal point, beginning with a closer look at some the prophecies made by both Old and New Testament prophets. The nativity story is one of journeys – to and from towns and cities, friends and relatives, distant lands, hostile powers. Often these journeys are triggered by signs of change, announcements of the birth of the Messiah, and these too are explored. Although obviously the birth of Christ is the fulcrum around which the narratives are centred, there are other births, both named –John – and unnamed – those slaughtered by Herod. Untold thousands of hymns, poems and stories have been woven around Christ's birth, and on Fridays and Saturdays we take a look at biblical examples of these. Finally, at the end of each week, we look at conversations which take place – with friends, with relatives, with God and with our innermost hearts.

The birth of Christ is a golden point in the overarching narrative of God's relationship with his children. By looking both back and forward as we move towards this point we can truly appreciate the anticipation with which this event was greeted, the nature of its happening and the transformation which was its result. Then we can turn and share with our neighbour our joy and hope in the future of God's kingdom.

To order a copy of this book, please use the order form on page 150 or visit **brfonline.org.uk***.*

Prayer is at the heart of BRF's work, and this special illustrated anniversary collection is a celebration of prayer for BRF's centenary year. It can be used in a range of different settings, from individual devotions to corporate worship. Including sections on prayers of preparation, seasonal prayers, and themed prayers for special times and hard times, it is the perfect daily companion to resource your spiritual journey.

The BRF Book of 100 Prayers
Martyn Payne
978 1 80039 147 5 £12.99
brfonline.org.uk

To order

Online: **brfonline.org.uk**
Telephone: +44 (0)1865 319700
Mon–Fri 9.30–17.00

Delivery times within the UK are normally 15 working days. Prices are correct at the time of going to press but may change without prior notice.

Title	Price	Qty	Total
Sharing the Christmas Story (BRF Advent book)	£8.99		
The BRF Book of 100 Prayers	£12.99		

POSTAGE AND PACKING CHARGES			
Order value	UK	Europe	Rest of world
Under £7.00	£2.00		
£7.00–£29.99	£3.00	Available on request	Available on request
£30.00 and over	FREE		

Total value of books	
Postage and packing	
Donation*	
Total for this order	

* Please complete and return the Gift Aid declaration on page 141.

Please complete in BLOCK CAPITALS

Title .... First name/initials .... Surname ....

Address ....

.... Postcode ....

Acc. No. .... Telephone ....

Email ....

Method of payment

❑ Cheque (made payable to BRF) ❑ MasterCard / Visa

Card no. ☐☐☐☐ ☐☐☐☐ ☐☐☐☐ ☐☐☐☐

Expires end ☐☐ ☐☐   Security code ☐☐☐   Last 3 digits on the reverse of the card

We will use your personal data to process this order. From time to time we may send you information about the work of BRF. Please contact us if you wish to discuss your mailing preferences **brf.org.uk/privacy**

Please return this form to:

BRF, 15 The Chambers, Vineyard, Abingdon OX14 3FE | **enquiries@brf.org.uk**
For terms and cancellation information, please visit **brfonline.org.uk/terms**.

Bible Reading Fellowship is a charity (233280) and company limited by guarantee (301324), registered in England and Wales

ND0322

Volunteer with BRF

At BRF we believe that volunteers have so much to contribute to our work and ministry as we support churches in their mission. We offer numerous opportunities, including the role of local church champion, whereby a volunteer shares the work of BRF with their local church.

Offering such a wealth of ministries for all ages, we are well placed to support churches in a way that is suitable for them and their context. Our volunteers working with church leadership are able to make a difference to the lives of others.

Our team of volunteers includes people from a variety of ages, denominations and backgrounds, each with varying skills. Some have a particular BRF ministry of interest while others are connected across all ministries.

The role is flexible to fit with each person's availability and varies in each setting. Some share information via their church notice sheet or have contact with specific individuals, such as children's or youth leaders or those working with older people. Others have contacts in their Churches Together network or denominational structures. Being well supported by BRF offers an opportunity to feel connected, as well as getting to know others in a similar role.

Angela in Wiltshire volunteered with the encouragement of her rector to encourage individuals and groups to get closer to God through regular study by highlighting the various BRF resources and updates in the parish newsletter.

Catriona Foster, one of BRF's volunteers, says:

I would sum up my volunteering with BRF as a rewarding and inspiring privilege. Not only is volunteering rewarding and enjoyable but recent research has shown that well-being is significantly improved when people are meeting and helping others and feel valued.

As volunteer Martyn Payne so helpfully expresses:

It is when we reach out to help others that we are most helped. This is the surprising equation of giving and receiving that lies at the heart of our faith in God.

If you or someone you know would be interested in joining the team, please contact **jane.butcher@brf.org.uk**

BRF needs you!

If you're one of our many thousands of regular *New Daylight* readers, you will know all about the rich rewards of regular Bible reading and the value of daily notes to guide, inform and inspire you.

Here are some recent comments from *New Daylight* readers:

'Thank you for all the many inspiring writings that help so much when things are tough.'

'Just right for me – I learned a lot!'

'We looked forward to each day's message as we pondered each passage and comment.'

If you have similarly positive things to say about *New Daylight*, would you be willing to help spread the word about these popular resources? Could you follow the example of long-standing *New Daylight* reader Beryl Fudge and form a *New Daylight* reading group, not to take the place of private prayer and reading but to share insights and deepen understanding? 'I've quite a few friends who also take the notes and we discuss them in the group,' says Beryl. 'There's so much in them every day. What I most value in *New Daylight* is the way they connect the Old and New Testament scriptures with what's happening here and now.'

It doesn't need to be complicated: every issue of *New Daylight* includes questions for reflection or discussion.

We can supply further information if you need it and would love to hear about it if you do form a *New Daylight* reading group.

For more information:

- Email **enquiries@brf.org.uk**
- Telephone BRF on +44 (0)1865 319700 Mon–Fri 9.30–17.00
- Write to us at BRF, 15 The Chambers, Vineyard, Abingdon OX14 3FE

Enabling all ages to grow in faith

At BRF, we long for people of all ages to grow in faith and understanding of the Bible. That's what all our work as a charity is about.

- Our **Living Faith** range of resources helps Christians go deeper in their understanding of scripture, in prayer and in their walk with God. Our conferences and events bring people together to share this journey, while our Holy Habits resources help whole congregations grow together as disciples of Jesus, living out and sharing their faith.

- We also want to make it easier for local churches to engage effectively in ministry and mission – by helping them bring new families into a growing relationship with God through **Messy Church** or by supporting churches as they nurture the spiritual life of older people through **Anna Chaplaincy**.

- Our **Parenting for Faith** team coaches parents and others to raise God-connected children and teens, and enables churches to fully support them.

Do you share our vision?

Though a significant proportion of BRF's funding is generated through our charitable activities, we are dependent on the generous support of individuals, churches and charitable trusts.

If you share our vision, would you help us to enable even more people of all ages to grow in faith? Your prayers and financial support are vital for the work that we do. You could:

- Support BRF's ministry with a regular donation;
- Support us with a one-off gift;
- Consider leaving a gift to BRF in your will (see page 154);
- Encourage your church to support BRF as part of your church's giving to home mission – perhaps focusing on a specific ministry or programme;
- Most important of all, support BRF with your prayers.

Donate at **brf.org.uk/donate** or use the form on pages 141–42.

Planning for the future

For I know the plans I have for you, declares the Lord, plans for welfare and not for evil, to give you a future and a hope.
JEREMIAH 29:11 (ESV)

Change is inevitable, and in recent years the idea of the unexpected has become so familiar one might even say that it is expected! In times of turmoil and unpredictability, it is a comfort and a blessing to hold these words dear. Where our plans may seem like an utter mess, God has a plan for us, and one that promises hope.

Jeremiah's words were written to Jewish people who had been forced by their enemies to settle in a foreign country. They were written to people who may have desired a quick fix, a promise of immediate safety and security. Instead, God promises that he has a plan, that he will give them a future and a hope.

Making plans for the long term can be intimidating, especially when thinking about the future and providing for our loved ones. But we can make those plans in the knowledge that God knows what lies ahead and is here for us in the present to show us into a hopeful future.

One important way to plan for the future is to make a will. Many people find this to be an anxious or complicated process, but it does not need to be. At BRF, we are reliant on fundraising activities, donations and gifts in wills to enable us to carry out our work. We are hugely grateful to everyone who remembers BRF in their will or who makes a donation in memory of a loved one.

After you have made provision for your family, friends and church, maybe you would kindly consider a gift of 1% in your will to help BRF. We always recommend visiting a solicitor to ensure that your will accurately represents your wishes. All you will need to take to your solicitor is our registered charity number, which is 233280.

If you would like any more information on making a gift to BRF in your will please do get in touch with our fundraising team on **01235 462305** or via **giving@brf.org.uk**.

We thank you for your support and your prayers.

The BRF fundraising team

NEW DAYLIGHT SUBSCRIPTION RATES

Please note our new subscription rates, current until 30 April 2023:

Individual subscriptions
covering 3 issues for under 5 copies, payable in advance
(including postage & packing):

	UK	Europe	Rest of world
New Daylight	£18.30	£26.25	£30.15
New Daylight 3-year subscription (9 issues) (not available for Deluxe)	£53.55	N/A	N/A
New Daylight Deluxe per set of 3 issues p.a.	£22.50	£32.85	£38.85

Group subscriptions
covering 3 issues for 5 copies or more, sent to one UK address (post free):

New Daylight	£14.55 per set of 3 issues p.a.
New Daylight Deluxe	£18.00 per set of 3 issues p.a.

Please note that the annual billing period for group subscriptions runs from 1 May to 30 April.

Overseas group subscription rates
Available on request. Please email **enquiries@brf.org.uk**.

Copies may also be obtained from Christian bookshops:

New Daylight	£4.85 per copy
New Daylight Deluxe	£6.00 per copy

All our Bible reading notes can be ordered online by visiting **brfonline.org.uk/subscriptions**

New Daylight is also available as an app for Android, iPhone and iPad **brfonline.org.uk/apps**

NEW DAYLIGHT INDIVIDUAL SUBSCRIPTION FORM

All our Bible reading notes can be ordered online by visiting
brfonline.org.uk/subscriptions

Title _____ First name/initials _____ Surname _____

Address _____

_____ Postcode _____

Telephone _____ Email _____

Please send *New Daylight* beginning with the January 2023 / May 2023 /
September 2023 issue (*delete as appropriate*):

(*please tick box*)	UK	Europe	Rest of world
New Daylight 1-year subscription	☐ £18.30	☐ £26.25	☐ £30.15
New Daylight 3-year subscription	☐ £53.55	N/A	N/A
New Daylight Deluxe	☐ £22.50	☐ £32.85	☐ £38.85

Optional donation to support the work of BRF £ _____

Total enclosed £ _____ (cheques should be made payable to 'BRF')

Please complete and return the Gift Aid declaration on page 141 to make your
donation even more valuable to us.

Please charge my MasterCard / Visa with £ _____

Card no. ☐☐☐☐ ☐☐☐☐ ☐☐☐☐ ☐☐☐☐

Expires end ☐☐☐☐ Security code ☐☐☐ Last 3 digits on the reverse
of the card

To set up a Direct Debit, please complete the Direct Debit instruction on page 159.

We will use your personal data to process this order. From time to time we may send you
information about the work of BRF. Please contact us if you wish to discuss your mailing
preferences **brf.org.uk/privacy**

Please return this form with the appropriate payment to:
BRF, 15 The Chambers, Vineyard, Abingdon OX14 3FE
For terms and cancellation information, please visit **brfonline.org.uk/terms**.

Bible Reading Fellowship is a charity (233280) and company limited by guarantee (301324),
registered in England and Wales

ND0322

NEW DAYLIGHT GIFT SUBSCRIPTION FORM

☐ I would like to give a gift subscription (please provide both names and addresses):

Title _____ First name/initials _____ Surname _____

Address _____

_____ Postcode _____

Telephone _____ Email _____

Gift subscription name _____

Gift subscription address _____

_____ Postcode _____

Gift message (20 words max. or include your own gift card):

_____

_____

Please send *New Daylight* beginning with the January 2023 / May 2023 / September 2023 issue (*delete as appropriate*):

(*please tick box*)	UK	Europe	Rest of world
New Daylight 1-year subscription	☐ £18.30	☐ £26.25	☐ £30.15
New Daylight 3-year subscription	☐ £53.55	N/A	N/A
New Daylight Deluxe	☐ £22.50	☐ £32.85	☐ £38.85

Optional donation to support the work of BRF £ _____

Total enclosed £ _____ (cheques should be made payable to 'BRF')

Please complete and return the Gift Aid declaration on page 141 to make your donation even more valuable to us.

Please charge my MasterCard / Visa with £ _____

Card no. ☐☐☐☐ ☐☐☐☐ ☐☐☐☐ ☐☐☐☐

Expires end ☐☐ ☐☐   Security code ☐☐   Last 3 digits on the reverse of the card

To set up a Direct Debit, please complete the Direct Debit instruction on page 159.

We will use your personal data to process this order. From time to time we may send you information about the work of BRF. Please contact us if you wish to discuss your mailing preferences **brf.org.uk/privacy**

Please return this form with the appropriate payment to:

BRF, 15 The Chambers, Vineyard, Abingdon OX14 3FE

For terms and cancellation information, please visit **brfonline.org.uk/terms**.

Bible Reading Fellowship is a charity (233280) and company limited by guarantee (301324), registered in England and Wales

You can pay for your annual subscription to our Bible reading notes using Direct Debit. You need only give your bank details once, and the payment is made automatically every year until you cancel it. If you would like to pay by Direct Debit, please use the form opposite, entering your BRF account number under 'Reference number'.

You are fully covered by the Direct Debit Guarantee:

The Direct Debit Guarantee

- This Guarantee is offered by all banks and building societies that accept instructions to pay Direct Debits.

- If there are any changes to the amount, date or frequency of your Direct Debit, Bible Reading Fellowship will notify you 10 working days in advance of your account being debited or as otherwise agreed. If you request Bible Reading Fellowship to collect a payment, confirmation of the amount and date will be given to you at the time of the request.

- If an error is made in the payment of your Direct Debit, by Bible Reading Fellowship or your bank or building society, you are entitled to a full and immediate refund of the amount paid from your bank or building society.

- If you receive a refund you are not entitled to, you must pay it back when Bible Reading Fellowship asks you to.

- You can cancel a Direct Debit at any time by simply contacting your bank or building society. Written confirmation may be required. Please also notify us.

Instruction to your bank or building society to pay by Direct Debit

Please fill in the whole form using a ballpoint pen and return with order form to:

BRF, 15 The Chambers, Vineyard, Abingdon OX14 3FE

Service User Number: | 5 | 5 | 8 | 2 | 2 | 9 |

Name and full postal address of your bank or building society

To: The Manager	Bank/Building Society
Address	
	Postcode

Name(s) of account holder(s)

Branch sort code

| | | – | | | – | | |

Bank/Building Society account number

| | | | | | | | | | |

Reference number

| | | | | | | | |

Instruction to your Bank/Building Society

Please pay Bible Reading Fellowship Direct Debits from the account detailed in this instruction, subject to the safeguards assured by the Direct Debit Guarantee. I understand that this instruction may remain with Bible Reading Fellowship and, if so, details will be passed electronically to my bank/ building society.

Signature(s)

Banks and Building Societies may not accept Direct Debit instructions for some types of account.

Enabling all ages to grow in faith

Anna Chaplaincy

Living Faith

Messy Church

Parenting for Faith

100 years of BRF

2022 is BRF's 100th anniversary! Look out for details of our special new centenary resources, a beautiful centenary rose and an online thanksgiving service that we hope you'll attend. This centenary year we're focusing on sharing the story of BRF, the story of the Bible – and we hope you'll share your stories of faith with us too.

Find out more at **brf.org.uk/centenary**.

To find out more about our work, visit

brf.org.uk

Sharing *the* Story *since* 1922